WINDOW OVER THE SINK

LIZ FLAHERTY

SINGING TREE PUBLISHING

WINDOW OVER THE SINK

Liz Flaherty

USA Today Bestselling Author

Window Over the Sink © Liz Flaherty, 2020
ISBN Ebook: 978-0-9971637-0-4
ISBN Print: 978-0-9971637-1-1

1st Edition, December 2020
Editor: Nan Reinhardt
Title Page Sketch: Marlene Chapin
Liz Flaherty Author Photo: Skyler Wilson
Cover Design and Formatting © Jacobs Ink, LLC., 2020

All Rights Reserved.
Singing Tree Publishing, 2020
Macy, Indiana

ABOUT WINDOW OVER THE SINK

*I*t's been nearly ten years since we retired. I'm still in the office Duane and the boys created for me. The seven quilts I promised to make have been completed. A few books. He has new knees and new guitars. We've had grief and loss in these years, occasional discontent, times of being alone even when we were together. We've also had a blessed amount of fun. Of music and laughter and family. Of the other side of being alone that comes of knowing we never really are.

Much has changed in those nine years and change, and much has stayed the same. At first, it seemed as if this book was a vanity thing. Or a thing for the grandkids to look at and think *Okay, Nana, what do you want me to do with this?* But in the end, like most other things in life that are worthwhile, it is a labor of love. A gathering of thoughts and dreams and memories.

Thanks for joining me on the journey.

DEDICATION

This collection is dedicated to all the people who have read Window Over the Sink, no matter where was published. Had it not been for your support, the column might have ended after a few weeks. Instead, it's gone on—sometimes sporadically—for over 30 years. Thank you so much. I hope you enjoy the book. Have a great week. Be nice to somebody.

FOREWORD

Journalists, particularly editors, are a cynical bunch. We question everything and everyone's motive. So that cynical trait cranked up to 11 when I picked up the telephone in the early 1990s—the exact date escapes me—to hear a woman's voice on the other end pitch her idea for a column.

Remember, this was before the Internet was "a thing," and social media that we have grown to love and loathe didn't exist. If you wanted to expose your writings to a mass audience, the local newspaper was the only game in town to accomplish that.

As news editor at the *Peru Daily Tribune*, I could afford to be choosy about the content that appeared in the limited space I had to fill every day.

And besides, I had enough experience to know that most people who fancy themselves as a writer have one good column inside of them, plus two or three more that aren't so good, and then they realize that writing is hard work, takes a lot of time, and they give up.

More fuel for the cynicism fire.

But Liz Flaherty was different. Over the telephone that day, she was persuasive and tenacious. She convinced me to give her a

FOREWORD

chance and publish, "Window Over the Sink." It was one of the better decisions I made as a young journalist and editor.

That first column was good, and there were more—lots more—to come. Liz is a writer who captures life in a rural Indiana county—the joys, challenges and heartaches. She writes with a flair and authority reminiscent of Erma Bombeck, but from a Hoosier perspective.

After a few years, we had moved on to new things. I moved to a bigger newspaper and eventually was forced to choose a new career thanks to the downsizing all news outlets are undergoing.

So I was pleased Liz reconnected with me over social media. And even happier to learn she had continued writing "Window Over the Sink."

What follows are decades of life experiences and thoughts that are as relatable today as they were when first published in the *Peru Tribune*. If a cynical editor liked them decades ago, I believe you'll like them today. —*Jeff Ward*

1
A ROOM OF MY OWN

It's been nine years since we retired. I'm still in the office Duane and the boys created for me. The seven quilts I promised to make have been completed. A few books. He has new knees and new guitars. We've had grief and loss in these years, occasional discontent, times of being alone even when we were together. We've also had a blessed amount of fun. Of music and laughter and family. Of the other side of being alone that comes of knowing we never really are.

DUANE and I had been married nearly 40 years when we retired, sharing space with all the attendant noise, mess, and drama that comes with having three kids, a house, and two jobs. By the time we started collecting our pensions, of course, the kids were grown and all the noise, mess, and drama were our own. We looked forward to all the time we were going to have to pursue our own interests and also ones we shared. He wanted to play golf and music. I wanted to travel and eat meals I hadn't chosen, shopped for, and cooked.

However…

Whenever anyone talks about retirement, there's always a "however." Have you ever noticed that?

Sharing a house during evenings and weekends was a piece of cake. We'd always done that well. Okay, maybe not always, but most of the time. Then suddenly, we were sharing it 24/7.

What were we thinking? I mean, really.

I still got up at 4:00 A.M. He slept until 8:00. I'd probably turned on the television three times in our married life—he didn't realize it had an off switch. I wanted to travel... oh, maybe once a month, to a different place every time. He wanted to travel once a year to Florida. He didn't care what he ate or when as long as there were pastries involved.

One of the interests I wanted to pursue was quilting. I'd promised the grandkids—all seven of them—I would make each of them a bed-size quilt when I retired. Not that I even knew how to make *one*, mind you, but that's a whole different story. However—there's that word again—quilting has quite a volume of mess involved with it (at least when I'm the one doing it), and no small amount of drama when it came to me learning how to cut things out. Especially triangles.

He still wanted to play golf, but his knees were wearing out, so it wasn't much fun. He still played music, but having me there all the time he was doing it bothered him.

It appeared we just might spend our happy golden years driving each other crazy. It was a learning time. With a steep curve. Oh, way steep.

But then my husband, with help from our boys, built an office/sewing room in the garage. It is the best of things, what Virginia Woolf wrote about in *A Room of One's Own*, an essay which I must own to never having read, but one that embraces the theory that "a woman must have money and a room of her own if she is to write fiction." If Ms. Woolf had been a quilter, she'd have expanded that list of Must Haves a bit.

Sometimes I feel guilty because I spend so much time out

here, but most of the time I'm just thrilled to have it. We are still together 24/7 (although the busyness of retirement makes that a gross exaggeration), but in addition to being a unit—the parental one, the grandparental one, the other halves of each other—we are also freely, happily ourselves. Virginia Woolf had it right.

2

GOALS AND SOMETIMES

I don't do resolutions, although I start each new year with some goals that sometimes I make (finish at least one book) and sometimes I don't (lose fill-in-the-blank pounds). I hope each year will be an improvement over the last one, which sometimes works out and sometimes not.

I used "sometimes" a little too often in that first paragraph, didn't I? But to tell the truth, it's an important word. If you say "always" or "never," you're committed to something whether you want to be or not.

Like "I would never say that." Sure, you would, if you were mad enough.

Or "I always wash the sheets every Monday." Unless I forget.

Or "I would never wear yoga pants to the grocery store." Yeah, you would. And hair curlers back in the day. And, if your nose is running and you're about to cough up a lung and you'd rather just stay in bed, maybe you'd wear your pajamas, too. (Lots of people do, even though they really shouldn't and I wish they really wouldn't.)

Or, my kids never did that. Okay. You go ahead thinking that.

Or, things were always better in my day. No. They weren't.

They were different and some things were better. Some things were awful.

Unless you say you've *never* done something that might be fun or exciting or mind-enhancing. Then you should add it to your list.

Or unless you say you're *always* glad to see someone or to help someone or to have a great conversation with them. Then you should hang onto those things and do them more often.

You can say you've never done or said something as long as you tack "yet" onto the end of the sentence.

You can say you always do or say something as long as you add "almost" in front of the always.

Often, though, you're better off with "sometimes," instead of committing to something you might not be able to accomplish. Or with "I'll try" instead of "I promise," because broken promises are much harder on both sides of any equation than trying and failing.

I need to interject here that I am kind of big on clichés and quotes—you may have noticed—and one of my favorites is *the only failure is in not trying*. Robert Kennedy said, "Only those who dare to fail greatly can ever achieve greatly." Even if greatness isn't your goal, daring to fail is an important part of any success.

There, do I sound pompous enough for you?

So, although I don't do resolutions, I have goals—finish another book, lose…a few pounds, laugh a lot, see good movies, cry some, read, see my family and friends every chance I get, stay healthy, volunteer.

I'll achieve all of them. Sometimes. And I'll keep trying.

Happy New Year.

3

THE GIFT OF GRIEF

It's Sunday afternoon when I write this, and the sun is almost out. How nice it is after two weeks of unremitting gloom. As it grows lighter outside, I grow lighter inside as well. Which is odd when you consider what I've been thinking about.

Grief.

We all see a lot of it in our lifetimes. When we're young and if we're lucky, we see it from afar. We see old people die and it's too bad, but...you know, they're old. Then, of course, comes the time when it's not from afar and the person who passes on isn't old. This is when we really find out about grief.

My grandmother died when I was seven, and even though it felt strange that she wouldn't sit at the table and drink from her cracked cup anymore, she was eighty-four. So I didn't grieve. Not really, though to this day, I think of Grandma Shafer when I see a cracked coffee cup. Then when I was eleven, a 10-year-old schoolmate died. Fifty years later, I still feel profound sorrow when I think of her. She was smart and funny and had so much to give here on earth that even now I have difficulty coming to terms with her death. But I couldn't identify the feelings I had about her passing, couldn't explain the tears that came to my eyes for years whenever I thought about Cindy being buried with her red cowboy boots.

When I was thirteen, I lost the only grandfather I'd ever known, and the hurt came in waves, like the throbbing from a bee sting. He died in June, and by the time school started, I'd gotten over the worst of it, but junior high was different than it might have been. Because grief wasn't far away anymore.

I've thought about it, off and on over the years. When my parents and father-in-law died, it hurt, but the grief part of it was far-flung, long-lasting, and unexpected. Life was so busy—we came home from Louisville after my father-in-law's viewing to go to my son's football game, then went back the next day for the funeral—that it just went on. I would see things, of course, that made me think of the parents we'd lost, and I kept Christmas-shopping for my mother long after she was gone. She was always hard to buy for, and I'd see things she'd like. And then, in the middle of J. C. Penney or Kmart, I would mourn, because I couldn't give them to her.

We often drive by the cemetery where my parents are buried. Sometimes we are past before I even think about it and occasionally I wave—"Hi, Mom"—and sometimes those bee-sting waves of hurt strike again. They've been gone for nearly 30 years; how can this be?

Sometimes we grieve for things—items irreplaceable but gone, or times—youth, when everything worked right and gravity was our friend, or even places—remember the Roxy and the railroad hospital and those spooky mansions on North Broadway? Now and then it is a state of mind we miss, or a conversation we wish could have gone on longer, or a friendship we wish we could go back and fix because we blew it big time.

I write a lot about gifts because, being the Pollyanna sort of person that I am, I think nearly everything is a gift. While I realize that this can be annoying to people who get tired of trying to be happy when they're just not, I find it much nicer than being unhappy when I don't have to. (Don't even try and straighten that sentence out—you can't do it.) But even I've never considered grief a gift. Until now.

Because until you love somebody or something, you can't grieve losing them. I wouldn't still miss my mother if she hadn't had such a positive and profound effect of my life. I wouldn't remember Cindy's red cowboy boots if I didn't recall their owner with affection. I wouldn't smile at cracked coffee cups if not for the grandmother who died when I was seven.

The buildings and the times and the friendships that are gone all leave remembrances and, in many cases, laughter, behind them. So, even though the Roxy is gone, I remember watching *Woodstock* there and singing along, from start to finish. And although the high school now climbs the Broadway hill in Peru, I remember walking quickly past the railroad hospital because it was scary looking. It is fun to remember that.

I remember boys who went to Vietnam. None of them were still boys when they came home, and some didn't come home at all. A part of me—and of everyone else who remembers the Vietnam era—mourns them still. But another part remembers how tall they walked and all that they gave. There was one who seemed stronger and better than the others and though I'm still sorry he had to go there and I regret the 14 months of his life he can never get back, I'm happy he came home safe. And married me.

So there you have grief. It tangles up with memories and joy and good things. It is, when all is said and done, a gift.

Till next time.

4
"...THE PRICE IS CHEAP..."

"Whatever the cost of our libraries, the price is cheap compared to that of an ignorant nation."
~~ *Walter Cronkite*

It's about the library.

You know where it is—it's the big old building on the corner of Main and Huntington. It's been remodeled in the past year so that the children's floor is bright and cheery and the tables and desks on the adult floor are refinished and waiting for you. There's room between the stacks to get around and plenty of places to sit and read the paper and decide if you really do want to read the book by a new author in your hands or if you want to stick to the tried-and-true.

If you have things to look up, there's a handy-dandy reference room back there to do it in. There are computers for everyone's use and all kinds of paper-and-ink books you can lose yourself in. More tables and chairs and pens and scrap paper to make notes on. One of those books, the *1875 History of Miami County*, led to my third or fourth book (you forget after while), *Home to Singing Trees*. Most of the history in my book came straight from that other big one, only I used my own words. (To have used someone else's is plagiarism. I learned that word early on. In the library.)

I've written something like 14 books now. Some with a large publisher, some with a smaller one, some released on my own. Writing books is one of those things that's kind of like a good pizza—it's everything it's cracked up to be. You probably won't get rich, but you're going to have a good time and you're guaranteed some satisfaction that comes from inside.

Before I wrote those books—and while I was writing them—I wrote a column for the *Peru Tribune*, "Window Over the Sink." It was the most fun I've ever had writing and I'd still be doing it if the climate in newspapering hadn't changed. I wrote feature articles, too, and had a few stories in magazines.

I didn't go to college. I didn't "know" anyone. But I had good teachers—thank you, North Miami—and I had the library. If it hadn't been for those two components, my life would have been very different.

Would it have been ruined? Nope. I'd still have my family, maybe the job I retired from, our home. Would it have been less? Yeah, I think so.

I wouldn't have written 14 books (and still counting). I wouldn't have written a couple hundred newspaper columns. I wouldn't have spoken to other would-be writers and said "yes, you can." Because I wouldn't have known it. I learned it from those teachers, whose names I can still recite to you 50 or so years later if you want to hear them, and from what's inside buildings like the one at the corner of Main and Huntington in Peru, Indiana.

It's easy to get a library card. Just take your ID in and fill out an application. And, if you live outside the city limits, pay $75.

Yes.

Now, personally, I don't think that's a big price for a year of being able to borrow books, audio-books, movies, and music from the library. However, that's just me. If my three kids still lived at home, it would be $300 for the four of us and the truth is we probably wouldn't have done it even if it meant they got to borrow books on their very own card and they got to take part in a Summer Reading Program that's just like that pizza I mentioned earlier—all it's cracked up to be. However, kids are weird; they have to eat and wear clothes and their shoe sizes change every two weeks—$225 for their library cards would have been a prohibitive expense.

But if we paid a tax to the library the way city residents do, it wouldn't be. I'm just like everyone else in that I don't *want* to pay more taxes, but the cost of supporting the library would be pretty small if it were spread out. And the payoff would be huge.

I know—yes, I really do—that there are those of you who won't want to pay a library tax because you're not going to use the library. You are the same ones who don't want to pay school taxes because you don't have kids in school. Well, just as I thank you for helping pay those school taxes so that all of those who attend county schools can do so, I would also thank you for paying a tax that would grant library privileges to county residents.

The kid over there in the third row in English class? He'll thank you, too, when he's writing his fourteenth book and his two-hundredth column because you and the other people who cared about the kids in this county paid those taxes. He'll talk to kids in classrooms and library meeting rooms and he'll say "yes, you can" because he came from somewhere that cared enough to take care of their own.

5

SILVER LININGS AND WOUNDED KNEES

*L*ast week, I read my column aloud at a writers' group meeting and one of the members mentioned how positive it was. It was, I agreed, and there were a couple of things about that. One was that I hadn't been feeling positive at all when I wrote it—I'd had to dig myself out of a deep pool of poor-me. The other was that if I'm the one writing it, it's going to be positive. Because, while I believe wholeheartedly in clouds—I'd better this spring, hadn't I? Clouds are nearly all we've had—I believe even more strongly in silver linings.

Sometimes it's really hard.

Sunday afternoon, we went to a long-term care facility to see a family member who is ill and needs care and treatment but who wants only to go home. Who isn't the person I know and love anymore, but yet he is. Each visit is like re-scraping a wounded knee that never fully heals. You limp in, and when you leave, the limp is more pronounced, the pain more intense.

Today it's cold and snowing, bitter white flakes that make your eyes sting and water. April's cruel wind is whipping around in true "gotcha" mode. I've heard this morning of yet another illness, another death, more regrets over a reluctant life change. If there's blue in the sky, you couldn't prove it by me. It is a melancholy, cloudy, sore-knee kind of day.

There are times in nearly every relationship, be it marriage, friendship, or family, that the connection wavers. When the bond must be reinvented to be either tightened or broken. Things that you wanted to always be the same are not. Things you wanted to change might do just that, but not necessarily in ways you'd hoped for. Whatever the outcome, it's never painless.

But, before Sunday afternoon was Sunday morning. We went to see our youngest grandson receive his first communion. It was a lovely service and the eight-year-olds looked—give me a Nana moment here—so stinkin' cute. Little girls in white dresses and little boys in vests and dress shirts and ties. The front of the church was crowded with parents and grandparents. Lunch afterward was my daughter-in-law's most excellent lasagna and good conversation. We left with exuberant little-boy hugs and reluctant ones from his adolescent brother. As grandparent days go, it was an extraordinarily good one.

After these days of cold and wind and all-consuming clouds, the sun will shine again—I hesitate to say it's guaranteed, but history indicates it. For those of us who need light more than others seem to, we'll see and feel hope with every sunrise.

Relationships will be what they will, but even ones that end leave good memories behind. They continue to occupy the "places in the heart" we all have. I can't, no matter how many Susie Sunshine columns I write, make all endings into happy things—that particular knee is going to hurt regardless—but there are new and wonderful beginnings, too. The trick is in finding them.

Plenty of writers (and meteorologists) talk about the clouds. They define them, differentiate between their types, and predict how long they are going to last. They do it well, and if you're in a bad place, it can undoubtedly lend comfort to know someone else is there, too.

But some of us are going to continue to search out the silver linings, to find positivity when, like I said above, it's really hard. We will continue to make lemonade out of the proverbial lemons and find something to laugh at even before our tears dry. We'll wear flip-flops in the snow because tomorrow will be better. I've been three days writing this column, but as I wrap it up, there are deer playing in the side yard and the sky is blue. It's going to be a good day.

6
...LET'S KEEP DANCING...

There are times—long, achy days of a bad knee and raging sinuses and throbbing finger joints—when I resent that I'm 50some and tumbling inexorably down the wrong side of the middle age slope. Is this all there is? I whine, channeling Peggy Lee. Have I worked all these years so I could afford to go more places and see and do more things just to learn I'm too old, too sore, and too damn tired?

I have time, now that I no longer preside over carpools, hold down bleachers, or operate a short-order kitchen and 24-hour laundry, to read all I want to. I have stacks of books and magazines beside my chair, along with a strong reading lamp, a spot for my coffee cup, and a blanket to cover my cold feet. However, if I sit in one spot for more than 15 minutes, I fall asleep. Most of my reading these days is done in the car, where I feed CDs of my to-be-read list into the player and "read" all the way to work and back. I love audio books, and listening to them makes my commute downright enjoyable, but there's something lacking without the reading lamp, the cup, and the blanket.

Now that tuition, six-boxes-of-cereal weeks, and expensive shoes and jeans are in my past, I could, if I was interested, buy much nicer clothing for myself. But gravity and years of eating too much and exercising too little have made buying clothes a nightmare instead of a pleasure.

At this stage of the game, we could spend our vacations in exotic places, where my husband could play golf as often as he wanted and I could lie in the sun reading and sipping drinks that come with straws, spoons, and umbrellas. Except my skin is already dry and taking on a leathery consistency and reading in the sunlight gives me a headache. Right before I fall asleep, that is.

There is time to write nowadays, especially in the lengthening evenings of spring. But I'm no longer sure I have anything to say. I used to think—only to myself, thank goodness—that I'd never have writer's block because I was way too full of hot air to ever run out of words. But the hot air has flattened and stilled and, in full panic mode now, I'm afraid I'll never get it back.

And then there are other times.

I spent a week in Vermont with my son's family. While my year-old grandson's parents worked, I got to spend my days with him. We crawled around on the floor, played with noisy toys, and squealed with laughter at nothing and everything. I read to him and he listened and watched my face with his father's bright blue eyes before falling asleep in my arms. I'd push back the recliner and pull the quilt his mother had made over us both and we'd nap together in warm and sweet contentment.

Another of my grandsons comes here on Thursday evenings while his brothers have Cub Scout meetings. He's newly housebroken and toddler-verbal and has his grandfather and me firmly wrapped around his sticky little finger. The half bath in our house is now his, since it's small and so is he, and the full bath is mine, which leaves grandpa without one. This is okay, though. Grandpa can use Nana's. If he asks first.

Each day for the last week I have walked my couple of miles and my knee has not protested. My hands, though stiff and a little swollen, have not ached. The roar of my sinuses has quieted to a dull murmur. The finches are putting on their bright yellow summer coats as they jabber at the feeders. Everywhere I look, lilies and crocuses and spiky green shoots are lightening the landscape. They're brighter now than they were in my 20s, when I was too busy to look at them properly.

This morning, as I drove to work, the quarter moon hung huge and orange in the eastern sky. God's thumbnail. Beautiful. I opened the car window and breathed deep of the soft pre-dawn air.

I'm grateful one more time that I no longer smoke. It's been three and a half years *(19 now—yay!)*, though I hardly ever count anymore, and there is an almost spiritual joy in having beaten it.

It's not so bad after all, this wrong side of the slope, where the colors are brighter and sharper and scents are sweeter and laughter is like music and grandchildren—anyone's; they don't have to be yours—are your reward for the difficult climb up the other side. Sometimes it's almost… yes, it really is… *better* than it used to be. Yeah, Peggy, that's all there is, and sometimes… most times… it's enough.

7
"...A NEW GAME EVERY DAY..."

"*Every day is a new opportunity. You can build on yesterday's success or put its failures behind and start over again. That's the way life is, with a new game every day, and that's the way baseball is.*"

~~ Bob Feller

THEY'RE BACK.

I don't mean spring flowers or myriad shades of green or much-needed rain or too much wind, though they're here, too. I'm talking about the boys and girls of summer who dot baseball diamonds and softball fields like the brightest flowers of all.

They wear caps and they chew massive wads of gum or something worse. They swing their bats around above their heads and scuff up the dirt at the bases so they can get their uniform pants good and dirty. Then they slide into base a few times to grind that dirt in so that it doesn't ever come completely out. That's what they're supposed to do; they're ballplayers.

The players' parents sit in the stands. They eat popcorn and swig on Coca Cola and talk to each other about what they should be doing but can't because Johnny has a game tonight and Jimmy has a game tomorrow night and Lucy plays on Friday nights and Sundays. They really get tired of sitting at baseball games, they tell each other, but wait a minute! Johnny's up to bat. The conversation changes, gets louder and more urgent. *Good swing! Just get a piece of it. You can do it. Good eye, Johnny. It's okay, just do the best you can.*

But parents do more than talk at ballgames. They knit, do paperwork, or fall asleep in their cars if the day's started too early and gone on too long. They work in the concession stand and hand out ice packs and free drinks after the game. They dig into their pockets when a kid really wants a Blow Pop but only has a nickel. Then they go home and wash uniforms and talk about how glad they'll be when it's all over for the year and they'll have time to do what the really should have been doing all along.

One summer, when my two sons were playing on separate leagues, I logged the number of baseball games I attended. Forty-two. That was 42 afternoons and evenings I could never get back. Good heavens, I had kids in baseball for 13 years. How many games was that?

In all honesty, I do have some regrets about the raising of my kids. I'm sorry I worried about how they wore their hair, that they wore high-tops with dress pants, that their rooms weren't clean. I'm sorry for the times I was unfair, the times I defended them when I shouldn't have and didn't when I should. I wish I'd been a smarter parent and a better example. I regret opportunities missed: when I should have shut up and listened or when I should have said encouraging words instead of their cruel opposite.

But I don't regret any of those 42 evenings and afternoons a year sitting at baseball games. Buying hot dogs and nachos for the family and calling it supper. Washing uniforms and handing them back to the kids before they were completely dry because it was time to leave for the next game. Talking and laughing with other parents and working in the concession stand when I'd already spent eight hours on my feet that day. I've never once been sorry for calling *Good eye, Just get a piece of it, Good job*.

Life stays rich when your kids are grown. You get to do things you haven't done in far too long. You can make travel arrangements for two, buy milk and bread once a week, and cook dinner with the surety no one's going to say, "I don't like that," and eat Cheerios instead. You can call your car your own, do laundry a couple of times a week instead of every day, and go for weeks on end without yelling, "turn that thing down." You don't have to share your makeup, the bathroom, or your clothes. You can spend money on yourself without lying awake suffering from guilt. No doubt about it—it's nice.

But sometimes it's too quiet. Sometimes there's too much alone time. Sometimes you'd like to sit on bleachers and yell *Good swing, Just do your best*. Because those are words you never regret saying and your kids always need to hear.

And because when it's over, when the fat lady of parenthood sings, neither baseball nor summer are ever the same again.

Enjoy every minute.

8

A REAL THING

"Love is an ideal thing. Marriage is a real thing."
~~ Johann Wolfgang von Goethe

ON SEPTEMBER 28, 1935, my parents went to a minister's house and got married. My dad wore a double-breasted suit and my mom had on a hat. They stayed married through the rest of the Great Depression and three wars, through the births of six children and the death of one at the age of three, through failing health and the loss of all their parents and some of my father's siblings. Dad died in 1981, Mom in 1982. They were still married.

From the viewpoint of their youngest child, who was born when they were in their early 40s and they thought they were finished with all that, it was the marriage from hell. I never saw them as a loving couple, never saw them laugh together or show affection or even hold hands. They didn't buy each other gifts, sit on the couch together, or bring each other cups of coffee. The only thing I was sure they shared was that—unlike my husband

and me—they didn't cancel out each other's vote on Election Day.

"Why on earth," I asked my sister once, "did they stay together all those years? Mom could have gone home to her family, even if she did have to take a whole litter of kids. Heaven knows Dad could have." (He was the adored youngest son and brother—he could do no wrong.)

Nancy gave me the look all youngest siblings know, the one that says, "Are you stupid?" When you're grown up, it replaces the look that says, "You're a nasty little brat." But I digress.

"Don't you get it?" my sister asked. Her blue eyes softened. So did her voice. "They loved each other. Always. They just didn't do it the way you wanted them to."

Oh.

I remembered then. When they stopped for ice cream because Mom *loved* ice cream. How they sat the kitchen table across from each other drinking coffee. How thin my dad got during Mom's long illness because "I can't eat if she can't." When they watched *Lawrence Welk* reruns together *loud* because—although neither would admit it—their hearing was seriously compromised.

And the letters. The account of their courtship. We found them after Mom's death, kept in neat stacks. They wrote each other, in those days of multiple daily mail deliveries, at least once a day and sometimes twice. When I read those letters, I cried because I'd never known the people who wrote them.

I have to admit, my parents' lives had nothing to do with why I chose to write romantic fiction. I got my staunch belief in Happily Ever After from my own marriage, not theirs. But how you feel about things and what you know—those change over the years.

As much as I hated my parents' marriage—and I truly did hate it—I admire how they stuck with it. I've never appreciated the love they had for each other, but I've come to understand that it never ended. I still feel sorry sometimes for the little girl I was, whose childhood was so far from storybook that she wrote her own, but I'm so grateful to have become the adult I am. The one who still writes her own stories.

But—and this is the good part—these are the things I know.

Saying "I love you" doesn't always require words. Sometimes it's being unable to eat because someone else isn't. Sometimes it's stopping for ice cream. Sometimes—and I realized this the other day when my husband and I were bellowing "Footloose" in the car—it's hearing music the same way, regardless of how it sounds to anyone else.

Marriage is different for different people. So is love. So is Happily Ever After.

Happy Anniversary, Mom and Dad.

9
I JUST WANTED TO THANK YOU...

My thanks to a wonderful website that offers writing prompts for helping me out today. Because, you know what? Sometimes it's really hard to come up with something to say. Writers, during practice-writing times and writing sprints and meetings with other writers who have the same...er...strange mind-workings as they have, often use prompts.

So, today, when my strange mind is as blank as it can be, I've chosen a prompt from the 51 offered on the website above. We'll see how it comes out.

Write a thank you letter to your favorite teacher.

This is a good one for me because I have a real soft spot for teachers. I think they're overworked, underpaid, and underappreciated. My favorite ones are the one I gave birth to and the one she married, but I'm not going to write them a letter. Kari would think I was dying and Jim would laugh at me.

But I do have a list of thank yous.

I was scared to death of my first-grade teacher. If I think about her very long, I can get scared again even now. But she

WINDOW OVER THE SINK

handed out the first Dick-and-Jane reader—and all the ones that followed it. I remember, so many years later, the first word on the first page: *Look*. Reading was the first thing I was ever good at, the first thing outside of family, my blue nylon dress, and a handful of dolls that I ever loved. I love it still. So I'm thankful to her.

Somewhere along the line, we were taught to write themes. Or essays. In my memory, it seems as if most people hated them, or at least dreaded them. I'm sure I sighed along with others, said I had no idea what I was going to write, and that I'd probably get a big red F anyway. But writing was the second thing I was good at. Or maybe I wasn't all that good at it, but I loved it. So I'm grateful to whomever assigned those themes and taught us the mechanics of beginning, middle, and end.

When I was a freshman, some evil force propelled me to take Latin. If you'd asked me at the end of that endless year what all I'd learned, I would have rolled my eyes and said, *"Amo, amas, amat, amamus, amatis, amant,"* conjugating the word for love. However, I'm still using what I learned in that single year of Latin. I like knowing where words come from, and I'm pretty sure a lot of mine came from Miss Fisher's room in the senior high hall.

We read Shakespeare in high school. Plays and sonnets. I felt like such a failure, because beyond watching Leonard Whiting and Olivia Hussey in the movie of *Romeo and Juliet*, I pretty much disliked everything of his I read. But if I hadn't read Shakespeare's sonnets, maybe I wouldn't have realized how much I liked Robert Frost's poetry. If I hadn't read Shakespeare's plays, I wouldn't have appreciated Jean Kerr and Neil Simon. That same year, we had to "cast" *Silas Marner* by cutting pictures out of magazines. I'm still casting books the same way. So, thanks, Mrs. Slauter.

I took two years of typing and a year of bookkeeping. My

bookkeeping skills were (and are) suspect, but I can keep a ledger well enough to get from month to month. I was among the slowest and least accurate typists, but I've written 20 books and several hundred essays using the touch system. Thanks a lot, Miss Boswell and Mrs. Johnson. You could have told a lot of stories beginning with, "If she could learn this, anyone can."

Mr. Heltzel taught about different kinds of writing. Mr. Andrews graded hard so that you knew what you did wrong. Mr. Huffman tried to teach me geometry and ended up passing me on effort alone because I didn't get any of it. Mr. Lewis gave me a C in U. S. History because no matter how much I loved history, I never got good at learning it. Mr. Wildermuth taught us algebra and humanity and standing up for what we believed.

The Fasts and the Pipers went to Washington, D. C. the week President Kennedy died. When they came back, they talked to the students, and we all felt like we'd been there, too.

There were bad times and places, too. Teachers who didn't like me and couldn't hide the fact. Even they taught me that not everyone's going to like you and it's something you need to live with; you don't like everybody, either. One or two who had me in tears. Crying in class taught me that just like in baseball, there shouldn't be crying in classrooms or workplaces. It needs to be done in private, because if the person who makes you cry sees you, they've won. Am I grateful to have learned that? No. But it's still a valuable lesson.

But there were so many more good than bad. I am reminded a little of the basketball seasons when I was in high school. Much of the time, our team lost more than they won, but it's the games themselves we remember more than the wins or losses. The playing. The players. The support. Teamwork.

School was that way. Teachers were, too. They were in the business of making productive grownups out of kids who may or may not have cared. Sometimes it didn't work, but they still played the game.

A favorite one, you say? No, there's no way I could pick one. So this is my letter to them all, and my thanks.

Have a good week. Be nice to somebody. Tell them Thank you.

10

ABOUT THE TRUTH

"For every good reason there is to lie, there is a better reason to tell the truth."
~~ Bo Bennett

It's no surprise to anyone that I spend far too much time on Facebook. Although I've learned the value of hiding posts that are upsetting, I haven't gotten used to the number of lies that are out there. Or to the fact that even in the face of irrefutable proof, the people who post the untruths and the ones who share those posts will spread those lies. It bothers me a lot.

I realized that I'd changed my mind about something. (And, no, the skies did not open with floods because I actually did that.) I always thought that of all the things that are bad for the world in general, greed was the worst. People are willing to let other people die because of greed, for heaven's sake—what could be worse?

Well, maybe not worse but just as bad might be lying about them. Shredding their reputations because you don't like them.

Having a great time at someone else's expense. Or lying *to* them —that's not good, either. Destroying faith and causing the kind of emotional and mental pain that leaves permanent scars.

There are people we expect to lie simply because that label has become attached to their professions. Politicians, lawyers, and salesmen all fall under that umbrella. Insurance companies, automobile manufacturers, and big banks do, too—since corporations are people, I guess they can be labeled as liars because so many of them fit the bill. Is it fair to color them all with the same brush? Probably not. Yet how do we decide whose word we're going to accept as truth?

If you choose *not* to lie, how can you convince people of your veracity?

If you've been lied *about*, how do you convince people of your innocence?

If you've been lied *to*, how do you find a way to trust again?

I'm pretty sure someone—maybe a bunch of someones—just said, "Who cares?" The truth is that what someone else thinks about us is their business, not ours. I understand, reluctantly, that not everyone is going to like me, but if they don't like me because of untruths someone else has told, that's hard to accept.

On the other side of the coin, is it always wrong to lie? I don't think so. I don't want someone telling me I look 75 when I'm only 67 even if it's true. I don't believe it's ever necessary to say, "Yes, actually," if someone is foolhardy enough to say, "Do I look fat?" If someone says, "Do you like my hair?" and I don't, I'm not going to tell them so, because where is the good in hurting someone for no good purpose?

And maybe that's my real question in this: Where is the good? While I understand that ill-gotten gains are still gains, are they worth the damage done along the way? If you win the game because you accuse your opponent of cheating, what have you really won? Or if you win because you cheated in some other way, does it really go into your win column or does it just make a mess of the score sheet?

So I ask again—the third time's the charm—where is the good? And go ahead—tell me the truth. I can take it.

11

AN OUNCE OF PERFECT

I was standing in the middle of my office, with the mess of office stuff on my left and the even bigger mess of sewing stuff on my right. The windows and door were open. The fifth episode of the second season of *The West Wing* was on television. The orioles were talking outside and our cat, Gabe, was just sitting there. He may have been a little cranky about the orioles, but he's old and he's a guy—maybe he was just cranky for general principles. I had coffee in my hand, fresh from the Keurig, sweetened and creamed to just the taste and color I liked. My husband wasn't here, but he'd kissed me goodbye when he left. We'd laughed about something and we'd danced in the hallway in the house before I came out.

I laughed out loud, in here with no one to hear me, and I can see my smile in the screen of the computer even now. The orioles in the yard are even more orange than they usually are. Birdsong is sweeter and flowers gorgeouser.

And there, just for a couple of minutes in my morning, life was perfect.

My friend Joe makes doughnuts. During the coronavirus quarantine, he's been delivering pastries to surrounding towns on certain days of the week. One town in particular was happy for his deliveries since their own long-time bakery was closed. The other bakery has opened back up now, so Joe stopped delivering to that town. He didn't have to. They didn't ask him to. But he wasn't interested in taking over someone else's playground.

For a moment in time, there was perfection in the world of local small business.

I like color. I like birds. I like rabbits and squirrels and deer in the yard. This morning, the cardinals, orioles, goldfinches, and blue jays—not to mention what I think was a bluebird but I'm not positive—are all over the place. I can see the rabbits down where they live and the squirrels scaling the cottonwood. No deer today, which is fine.

The scene out my office window is perfect. Just now.

My friend Terri gave me ten bags of fabric. Yes, ten. Since I already have...much fabric, I don't need to get into those ten bags all at once. They're sitting over there on the sewing side of the room. And it's like having a Christmas tree in May. Each of those bags is a gift and I don't know the contents. When I need something new, something uplifting, I open a bag. I make plans for the pieces of fabric in the bag. Masks, or one beautiful piece I'm going to be wearing as a summer top—if we ever actually get summer—or the center of a quilt block.

There is nothing except the fabric and the plans for it and who can be made happy by what is done with it. Happy's good. Passing it on is even better. Opening that bag makes for several perfect moments.

There are drive-bys going on for high school graduates. This morning I watched a video of North Miami staff sending their students off for the summer with signs and waving. Dry eyes weren't an option if you were watching.

It was perfection in a time of pain and loss.

As part of a lifestyle, a vocation, or an avocation, I think perfection is overrated—possibly because I've always known I had neither the patience or the necessary skills to achieve it. I'm a great fan of *pretty good, good enough,* and *okay.* If something was fun, productive, and no one was hurt, that's as close to perfect as I need.

I remember a customer showing me a bubblegum card with a a young Mickey Mantle on it. I was so impressed because it was really old and it was…you know…Mickey Mantle. But he said it was worthless because it was so imperfect. The corners were crumpled and it was faded and it looked…old. All I could think was, *Yeah, but it's Mickey Mantle.*

And yet. And yet I can still appreciate those moments of perfection. And talk about them, remember them, and be glad they happened. So, once again in my best Pollyanna Whittier voice, I'm asking you to look for the perfect, enjoy it, and store it up so that when 2020 is in the past, you will remember more than darkness. More than division. More than haters hating and people dying and high school seniors having to grow up at least a semester before their time.

I hope you'll remember that while churches were silent, the people who attend them still worshiped. That while school buildings were closed, teachers (and parents!) still taught and students still learned. Don't forget bright orange birds, graduates not in the least lessened by not being able to march with their classmates to "Pomp and Circumstance," and health care and other essential workers who stepped up Every Single Day of the quarantine. Remember always that in the midst of all that was bad, there were also moments of perfect in every day.

12

THE AMETHYST AND AVERY'S HEART

On a recent evening, I spoke at the Black Dog Coffee House in Logansport. It was a big step outside my comfort zone, and, never confident, I wore my favorite amethyst necklace for luck. I saw some friends, Savanna and Bryce, before the talk. They introduced me to Avery, their little girl. Before I "went on," Avery gave me a little red heart to keep. I slipped it into my pocket, pushed the comfort zone into the corner, and started to talk.

I wondered how I would fill an hour because, you know, I'm just not that interesting. But it was something like an hour and twenty minutes later that Scott Johnson suggested we wind it down. A responsive audience made the whole experience so much fun I'm still thinking about it days later, still reaching up to touch the stone in my necklace and remembering. Still stroking my thumb over Avery's heart.

I write romance novels, and when I finish a book, I tend to think of the hero and heroine staying where I left them, probably sitting on the couch in front of the fire smiling into each other's eyes. As time goes on, they'll have children, she'll gain a few pounds, he'll need bifocals. The cat and dog in the picture will change. The carpet on the floor will go over to hardwood and then on to a large area rug.

But it will be—I hesitate to use this word because how it sounds isn't what I mean—static. Although they'll argue, because that's what couples do, and sometimes there'll be a lonely space between them there on the sofa, there won't be big unhappy things. No one will throw anything. No one will cheat or lie or withhold love from the other. No one will say, Do you want a divorce? Or even the slightly less devastating, Do you think we should separate for a while? Because that kind of thing doesn't go on in happily-ever-after, right?

Come on, am I right?

No. Of course I'm not.

Because it doesn't work that way, does it? There may be people who are in love every day, who never have times of coolness and distance with their friends, and who don't occasionally wonder what they were thinking when they signed up for parenthood, but they aren't people I know.

The heart Avery gave me is smooth red plastic, but in reality, our hearts have all kinds of cracks and scars on them. The seams are zig-zaggy where all the pieces wouldn't go back together right and some of the color is worn off from being broken so many times. But, scars and all, we're still in love and we still cherish our families and friends. Our kids—and their kids—are the reason we breathe. Our hearts, battered as they are, are what keep us connected.

We all know, don't we, that happiness, including the ever-after kind, is comprised of moments. Not decades or years or even months. It's not in the grand gesture or the public avowal or the get-a-room variety of public displays of affection—not that kind of moments. It's not even in those deepest ones that stay in your heart forever, when children are born or graduate or marry. When grandchildren are born. Or when grief creates a new visceral bond between you that you hoped never to feel.

Rather, happiness is what comes in the middle of despair and saves us. It's a small brushstroke on the big picture, where the sun peeks between the clouds to reassure us that we'll see it again soon.

For me, it is in the amethyst, that makes me happy and makes me feel lucky when I wear it. I remember standing there in Gilbert's when Duane bought it for me, and crying months later when I thought I'd lost it. I remember Duane standing in the kitchen with it draped over his hand when he found it, just looking at me and laughing. The day of the talk, Denee Douglass both did my hair and fastened the necklace's clasp for me because I can't anymore. It was a moment of friendship in the middle of the day.

It is in the little red plastic heart. A week later, I smile every time I think of it and Avery's smile-lit face. The heart lives in my wallet and I see it every time I open it. She gave me the gift in what was probably a thirty-second meeting. I can't count the thirty-secondses of happiness it's given me in the days since.

So, I wish you all happily-ever-afters. That promise is one of my favorite parts of writing romance. Even more, though, I wish you many happy moments—thirty-second segments that provide that bit of sun, the brushstroke you need to complete your big picture, and the kind of joy that comes with an amethyst necklace and a little girl's heart.

13

BETWEEN TWO SHADES OF BLUE

*L*ast night—Thursday—I sat in the living room and started a disgruntled column on why I have the winter blues. Even though we haven't really had winter to speak of yet and even though I don't really have the blues, I just couldn't think of anything new and different to say.

But now it's Friday morning and sunrise is out there, brilliantly red and pink and purple. The lightening sky in the west is the most gorgeous shade of blue. I looked on a color chart and it was somewhere between Olympic and Azure. By the time I looked up from the chart, it was different.

Every time you look away, something changes. Seasons come and go. Decisions made in the heat of a moment will be wrong when the intensity cools. Or not. Sometimes they are stunningly, life-changingly right.

I'm not sure where I'm going today, so hope you'll just come along for the ride. A friend, Debby Myers, mentioned that I used the words "always" and "never" a lot. In the essay she was referring to, I did. For that particular one, where I was talking about myself, it was pretty much right. I wrote about "sometimes" less than a month ago, and that's still my preferred mode of promissory travel, but when we're talking about ourselves, we can often be certain enough of our own responses

But we don't know others well enough to sticky-tape those words to them. We don't know what's going to happen in their lives between Olympic and Azure blues.

When I wrote *The Happiness Pact* back in 2017, I had a lot of help. Libby had severe clinical depression. She was also a stargazer, and I needed a way to work that into her story that I couldn't figure out on my own. Danna Bonfiglio, a friend of my kids from elementary days on and an English teacher at the school they all attended, told me Venus had been her guardian planet when she was a kid. Still was, come to that.

During an online conversation, she said, "I used to sing that Frankie Avalon song when I was a kid...if I liked a boy, I would talk to her [Venus] about it. I never told anybody that before. I remember taking a summer astronomy class at IUK, and we looked at Venus through the telescope. I was so excited."

So was I. Venus became Libby's guardian planet, watching over her heart and bringing her through the rough parts.

And there are always rough parts.

Over a year ago, Danna was diagnosed with pulmonary thrombosis. She needed a lung transplant, but her time on earth ran out before it could happen. She passed away January 13, surrounded by her family. Mourned by so very many.

In large part, writers are able to write emotion because they've felt it first or because someone else has somehow given it to them as a gift.

When Danna gave me Venus to use in a story and to absorb how much having that guardian planet meant to her, that emotion became a healing agent for Libby's depression. It was a particular stream of tenderness in a tough story to tell. In her 20-

some years of teaching, Danna was the guardian of hundreds of young hearts as well as the sharer of information. She had a wide streak of tenderness. She is the guardian of her students and the others she loved yet. She and Venus.

———

FOR NEARLY EVERYONE I KNOW, there has been much loss in the recent past. I don't know what to say about it that hasn't already been said over and over. Loss and living with it are those rough parts. They run over our hearts and leave them aching and bleeding, with empty, torn places—that's fact. Another fact is that before we can heal, we have to ache and bleed.

But sometimes there'll be a sky like the eastern one this morning, full of promise and brightness. And, between the blues in the west, something will change, and we'll laugh and see brightness in the gloom. Sometimes. And, we hope, we'll begin to heal.

Have a great week. Be nice to somebody.

14

BLESSED ARE THE CURIOUS

"*Blessed are the curious, for they will have adventures.*"

I don't know who said it first. I saw it on Facebook this morning as I was dodging my way through, avoiding name-calling and cruelties and half-truths on my way.

Isn't it the coolest thing? That saying, I mean, not Facebook. There are lots of ways to apply it on Facebook alone, since I already mentioned it. Telling the truth and avoiding name-calling and other cruelties are adventures I wish everyone would give a shot, but I don't expect that to happen.

Back to the quotation, though, how much could we learn if we only remained curious, and what great adventure is there than learning about things we don't know or understand?

When I was a kid, I read Gene Stratton-Porter books. She was an Indiana author who came from Wabash County and wrote a longer list of books than I could find. I read and enjoyed many of her novels, but she wrote about nature, too. She had an interesting life and, more important to me, she was an interesting person. A friend and I visited Porter's Cabin at Wildflower Woods on Sylvan Lake near Rome City. We ended up spending most of the day there, being curious. By the time we left, we understood her and her motivations. We were enriched by the experience.

Somewhere among the greats in my family tree, I had an uncle who committed suicide. I don't remember his name and I never heard anything about him. The earlier generations of my family—I imagine much like many others—didn't talk much about things. About feelings or pain or why anyone did what. While I understand that that was just the way of things, I wish I knew more. I am curious. One place that curiosity led me showed me that the uncle who'd killed himself had lost a child as a toddler less than a year before his own death. It made me understand. It wasn't exactly an adventure, but it was something important in the family's history that people had been, I assume, ashamed of. They should have been empathetic instead. Parenthood is the greatest adventure of all—having it taken away is the worst nightmare.

When I wrote *Home to Singing Trees,* I researched for a couple of years. Although I have no patience with microfilm or microfiche, there are a ton of local history books in every library around. If I'd used every "can you believe this?" piece of lore I'd found in those books, I'd never have gotten the book written. The good thing is that long after I had the information I needed, I kept reading. I grew up near Gilead, population somewhere in two digits, and things happened there. Also in every other wide spot in the road in Miami County. I know—I read about them all.

Wondering about things leads me to history, as you can tell. I've found peace in old cemeteries, glory and indescribable pain on battlefields, and made "oh, this is why" discoveries in places where the subjects of my curiosity grew up and lived.

But it doesn't have to be history. Seeing how things are made is interesting, too. Learning to make them yourself is an adventure. I want to learn to make soap someday. My mom did, with lye and some kind of hot grease. She put it in a big old metal dishpan and cut it into bars and did laundry with it—in a wringer washer. Oh, history again...

There are classes all around where you can make jewelry, ones where you can make greeting cards, fairy gardens, and countless other things. Artists at Gallery 15 and the Miami County Artisan Gallery offer classes and private lessons in any medium you can think of. You may not be good at them (you don't want to see my Wine & Canvas attempt), but you'll have a good time and it will be an adventure.

I need to find a class in how to write a column without skipping all over the place, but no one's offering that one...

Back to curiosity and adventure. Being curious means finding out the truth about something. Adventure means exploring it once you do. In this time of soaring untruths and bitter division, it's so very important to look beyond what you think you know. It's also important to go beyond what you do know so that you can learn about things. And explore them.

So, go forth and be curious. Have a good week. Be nice to somebody.

15

TURKEY, JOY, AND A SMALL GLASS OF BEER

"Let us be grateful to the people who make us happy; they are the charming gardeners who make our souls blossom."
~~ *Marcel Proust*

AUNT NELLIE WAS MY GREAT-AUNT. She was born in 1892, loved and married two men, and never had any children. She was the other side of the coin from my grandmother, who'd undoubtedly been the Good Daughter, and even though I loved them both, I worshiped the ground Aunt Nellie walked on.

My mother's side of the family were all teetotalers, but when my brother-in-law asked Aunt Nellie if she'd like a beer, she said, Yes, she wouldn't mind a small glass. I don't know that she ever drank beer again, but she did indeed enjoy every drop of that "small glass." Where Aunt Nellie was, there was always laughter.

We used to go to her house for Thanksgiving. I'm not sure how many of us were there. It seemed like dozens at the time, but the number was probably closer to 25. She lived in a pretty little Cape Cod house on a pretty little street in Goshen, Indiana, and she had...oh, even in memory, it thrills me...she had a step stool you could sit on and the steps pushed out in front! She also had a finished basement with its own kitchen! In the living room part of the basement, there was a cabinet Victrola with a stack of records. They were tinny and scratchy and it was hard to get them going the right speed with the crank, but there was such safety lying on the rug listening to Bing Crosby and Dinah Shore.

Even though I grew up on a small farm, the only time we ever had turkey was on Thanksgiving. I'm pretty sure I ate my weight in it every year. I loved eating whatever I wanted and never having to touch the squiggly red stuff that slid out of the Ocean Spray can. The dessert table was impressive, to say the least, and it was pretty much stripped by the end of the day. Even then, leftovers went home with each family, and the feeling of fullness and warmth would go on with turkey and noodles the next day.

I imagine being poor was a key player in my satisfaction with Thanksgiving, but that's really neither here nor there. What matters are the memories and the lessons Aunt Nellie left behind. She was somewhere in her 80s when she died. She'd been packing for a trip to Grand Rapids with friends when she passed away. Grief created a hard, empty place in my chest at the loss, and I just knew I'd never get over it. However, at the funeral the officiating pastor mentioned her preparing for her trip and said she'd been just as ready to go to heaven as she'd been to go to Grand Rapids. My grandmother, who'd loved her younger sister even more than we did, said she thought if she'd had her choice, Aunt Nellie would rather have gone to Grand Rapids. Laughter softened the grief and added one more rung to the memory ladder.

Aunt Nellie was one of the first people I thought of when I became a Harlequin Heartwarming author. She'd have loved the line's premise, its joy and sense of family, and its humor. She'd have also told everyone at the beauty shop all about her niece, the author. Knowing that reminds me again of how lucky I was to have her.

Happy Thanksgiving to all. If you have that small glass of beer, be sure to enjoy every drop.

16

CHANGES

Do you love old music? Well, it's not old to me—it's the stuff from the 1950s and '60s and '70s that has filled spots of need and longing and depth within the hearts of Boomers since those first days of Bill Haley and the Comets. I love listening to it. Elvis and John Lennon and the Eagles and more than I could list even if I had all day. Fairly frequently, new performers will cover some of the songs that have filled my playlist for 50-some years. I'm always vaguely resentful when they do. They don't do it right, I think. They emphasize the wrong words. It seems as if they sing, not from their diaphragms and their hearts the way my husband says you need to, but just from the sheet of paper in front of them on a music stand.

But, sometimes…don't you just love being wrong? Disturbed's version of Simon and Garfunkel's "The Sound of Silence" left me in awe. And covered in chill bumps. And listening to it again. And again. And again.

It made me think of things that are life-changing. Things that you never expect to be. That you don't realize until much later. I'm going to list some of my own. I'd love to know yours, too, because even though I like talking about myself as much as the next person, I know I'm not that interesting.

I remember walking into the front room at Keller Kleaners to see the guy I was dating and meeting a friend of his. Who didn't like me at all. We'll be married 49 years in May. At some point, he decided he liked me after all. We've had a lot of life-changing days in those years. I love it when we see most of them on holidays.

I was in the fifth grade the year Kennedy became president. We learned about elections, about voting, about parties. We had a template of the voting machine and we held our own presidential election in the classroom. My candidate lost, which I quickly became used to, but he won the "real" election, and even though I didn't become political then, I did develop a fascination with the process. Until recent years, I loved it.

On February 9, 1964, the Beatles were on *The Ed Sullivan Show*. It was amazing. I don't have a musical bone in my body, but that was when I first found out it wasn't the body that counted so much with music as it was the heart. (Refer to paragraphs above…)

On November 22, 1963, the president I'd voted for in that classroom election was assassinated. It was one of those days, like 9/11 and the day the Challenger broke apart, that I can remember in snapshots that are as clear and painful as if they happened just yesterday.

Another November, I went on a Christian retreat that solidified my faith.

At some point in time, I heard the song "Hallelujah."

Someone called me a snowflake.

An editor called and said, "We want to buy your book."

Twice, I got jobs I'd coveted, which led to friends I still have.

I asked the then-editor of *Peru Tribune* how he'd feel about me writing a column. I'd call it "Window Over the Sink."

All 10 of those things I listed—are you still reading?—altered the course of the rest of my life. There have, of course, been a ton of others. Births, deaths, immeasurable loss, indescribable joy.

While I was writing this—and changing its course several times, as usual—I watched a video of "Dancing Queen" from *Mamma Mia*. I remembered when our high school basketball team went to the semi-state. I thought about my oh-so-conservative brother streaking way back when. I made coffee and recalled the first time I ever had a cup of Green Mountain Nantucket Blend.

And I realized something, sitting here at my cluttered desk as I look out at the sun shining down on the telephone poles and turning them white. Every day offers us the chance to change things, doesn't it? To change ourselves. It doesn't have to be huge and dramatic or excruciatingly painful or even extraordinarily happy.

It can be as little as listening to someone new sing an old song and just killing it—and finding out you can be totally wrong about something and the world doesn't turn on you.

Or singing "Dancing Queen" with Meryl Streep really, *really* badly and feeling good when you're done. Kind of "I Am Woman—Hear Me Roar"-ish.

It can be conversation. Or kindness. It can be tolerance. Or lending a helping hand—or receiving one. Or just listening to that "sound of silence."

It doesn't really take much to change a life, whether it's yours or someone else's. Think about it.

Have a good week. Be nice to somebody. It might change their life. Or yours.

17

THE EMPTY CHAIR AND THE SILENT VOICE

I've written about grief before, about what a gift it is because of the love that came before the loss. I still mean that, but I left too much out of what I said before. While I didn't make light of the pain of loss, I probably didn't address it, either.

Grief is hard. I tried to think up some better words, to be more articulate, but there really isn't a better one. It's just hard.

When you've gotten through a day and you haven't cried or had regrets or thought too long about how you'll never see the person you lost again in this lifetime, you might think the worst is over. You sleep through the night and wake without the familiar feeling of dread that goes with mourning and you think it's a brand new day. The sun still comes up. The first cup of coffee's still the best one of the day. You will be strong today. You will laugh and mean it, be productive. You'll be yourself again.

But then there's a memory lying in wait to trip you up. A picture or a song or the sound of the guy's voice who does the morning news. And you won't be yourself at all. You can't. Because the person you've lost is still gone and you're not his sister or son or parent anymore. The picture of every slice of life from here on out will have a blank space in it. So will your heart. And, no, you can't see it as a brand new day. Not yet, not when today is just like yesterday and the grief is still heavy and dark and unbearable.

If you're like me, you've probably read about the stages of grief and you know you have to go through most of them or all of them. What you don't know is how long they are going to take. My friend Nan Reinhardt lost her sister and months later was saying, "I can't get over it. I know I should, but I can't."

There is no "should" because there is no timeline. No criteria for comparison, no depth meter that says my grief is greater than yours or vice versa. Saying "I know how you feel" is always a mistake because everyone's grief is different. You might know how you would feel, but not how someone else does. How another person mourns isn't open to criticism or measurement. It is, however, open to friendship, to sharing memories, to laughing even if you're crying at the same time.

I'm convinced laughter is the greatest healer of all. While I still can't bear the idea that my brother is gone, I can laugh out loud at Jim's recounting of a streaking adventure. At an IOU for 10 cents that Tom's not sure he ever paid back. At the memory of Dan reciting "Fuzzy Wuzzy Was A Bear" at school. (He never saw the humor in that one.) At the fact that when the four remaining siblings are together, it is still as if we grew up in different houses because our memories vary so widely.

Even as we laugh, though, we're conscious of the empty chair and the silent voice.

This isn't a good place to end a column on grief, is it? That's because there isn't a good place—there is no solution to grief. Just the hope that humor and its brother time will continue to ease the sorrow that's still in the deep middle dark times.

If you're there, too, I hope you have the support of friends and family who may not be there themselves but want to be with you while you are. I hope you have good memories and the laughter that goes along with them. I hope you soon find your way through the stages until the morning comes that really is the start of a brand new day.

Have a good week. Thanks for listening.

18

PAY ATTENTION

Do you have grandparents? Well, of course, we all have them, don't we? Let me tell you about some of the ones in my life.

Grandpa Shafer was born in 1869. He was a farmer and he went blind from glaucoma. He died when I was two. My sister remembers sitting with him in the car while Grandma was at the store and that most of the time he lay on the couch in the living room. He and Grandma got married in the 1890s and had two sons and seven daughters. They lost two babies who were buried in the garden and their oldest daughter, Amy, who died in 1918 during the influenza epidemic.

When the house was on fire, Grandma carried the treadle sewing machine down the stairs. She always drank coffee out of a cracked cup and saved the others for company. She spent time in her rose garden alone. I was way down on the list of grandchildren and I don't remember having any kind of relationship with Grandma.

It wasn't until years after her death, when I'd become a mother, that I realized the anguish she'd survived. Amy had been in her early 20s when she died, the babies had never drawn breath, and Grandma lost the man she loved most of her life. I hope she found comfort in the rose garden.

Grandpa Neterer started as a farmer, then went to work at a band instrument factory in Elkhart, Indiana. They lived in the village of Bunker Hill, which hadn't really been "in town," but town grew up around them. However, he still went barefoot and kept a few chickens out back. They had city water that tasted awful, but the well pump was in the side yard. If you were a country kid and got a drink of water at Grandma and Grandpa Neterer's, you went out there to get it—you couldn't stand what was in the house. They had a barrel of rain water, too, that felt like silk when you ran your hand through it. And a strawberry patch and raspberry bushes and sometimes you could smell honeysuckle.

Some of my grandsons have lost grandparents, but I remember one time when Skyler was intent on pulling the heads off every flower his "Mimi" had. She waved a dismissive hand and said, "It's just flowers. They'll grow back." The day Connor was born, we got to the hospital when he was just a few hours old. His paternal grandfather was already there—for the third time.

Two more grandsons make maple syrup and ride horses with their other grandparents.

One of my daughters-in-law sewed with her grandmother. Another visited hers in New York and heard fascinating stories from her.

My mother-in-law lost her mother when Mom was three. Her grandmother raised her. It wasn't an easy life, ever. At one point, Mom carried the mail on horseback.

I'm not writing this to tell you how important grandparents are, but to tell you—not for the first time—to harvest the memories they bring with them. My generation remembers the 60s much better than the textbooks will relate. We still remember the words to the songs, the shock and liberation of peaceful protest. I remember borrowing money in my name to establish my own credit and Peru Trust Bank sent the invoice to my husband.

My parents lived through the Great Depression and World War II and their parents remembered World War I. Duane's and my generation lived under Vietnam's dark shadow. He served and I waited. My grandmothers couldn't vote until one was in her 30s, the others her 40s.

I wish I'd asked more questions while they were here. I wish I'd paid more attention. I hope you ask everything you can think of and write down the answers. Take pictures that capture the faraway look in their eyes. And while you're doing that, listen for more than words—listen to how they felt when their history was happening. You won't find that in a textbook, either.

Have a great week.

19

DON'T MISS IT! DON'T EVEN BE LATE!

*L*ast night my husband and I went to the fair. We didn't get there until about eight o'clock. We were going to get something to eat, take a quick run around the exhibits, and be home in an hour and a half or so.

After all, we said, the fair Isn't What It Used To Be. We don't ride on the rides anymore, or play the games offered on the midway. Since our kids are all out of school, we can't even look up many of their friends 4-H exhibits anymore. It's just not the same.

When I was a little kid, a hundred or so years ago, the fair took place during the week of my birthday. On one day during the week, not necessarily my birthday, my mother would work in one of the food places at the fair and I would take my birthday money and run wild until she came and found me and told me we had to go home.

I never got to run wild very often, so I always took full advantage of it. I picked up duckies and won wonderful little bamboo canes. I laid nickels on numbers and went fishing with the little crane and threw more nickels at shell-shocked goldfish. One year, I talked one of my brothers into taking me on the

Bullet—I was scared to death to go by myself—and I lost all my money while I was on it and a whole bunch of cotton candy and caramel corn as soon as I stumbled away from it a couple of traumatic minutes later.

It was probably a good ten years before I braved the Bullet again, and then only after I'd left all my worldly goods with someone intelligent enough to remain on the ground and before I'd had time to eat anything I stood a good chance of losing the hard way.

The fair remained wonderful through my teenage years. There was nothing more romantic than smooching with someone on top of the Ferris wheel or toting home a hideous teddy bear won for you by someone. Another side to that romantic thing was fighting with someone while you were there and having to ride home with your girlfriends while you cried and said you never wanted to see him again. Ever. (Note from 2020. If this happened, I don't remember it. That's either a sign my memory's truly gone or indicative it wasn't all that serious of a relationship.)

But then things kind of changed. The only time we went to the fair was on family day when the rides wouldn't entirely break the bank and the only ones who rode were our kids. Except for when their dad rode the Bullet with them while I held everyone's money and a good supply of wet paper towels.

Pretty soon the kids were going to the fair without us. We would manage to go out one night to eat pork chops and do a quick run through the exhibits and get home in an hour and a half. All the way home, I would complain that It Just Wasn't What It Used To Be.

Until last night.

When we spent some quality time talking to people we hadn't seen in years and remembered how much we miss them.

When I stuffed myself with a tenderloin the size of a dinner plate that tasted just as wonderful as they did that hundred years or so ago I mentioned up there.

When we walked, not ran, through the exhibits and marveled at the talent and hard work of those doing the exhibiting. When we looked up our favorite 4-H members' entries and crowed proudly at their blue ribbons.

When we strolled through the midway and smiled at laughing babies in strollers and their excited siblings on the rides. Their parents waited patiently and tiredly with the strollers, talking to others doing the same, and we knew what they were saying. "The fair just isn't the same anymore."

When we sat in hard chairs in a big tent and watched dozens of cloggers doing their thing. The noise from their shoes was deafening. And rhythmic. And pretty-sounding. The bobbing black ponytail in the front row was captivating, nearly as much so as the smile on the face of the ponytail owner.

Exhibits. Smiling cloggers. Laughing babies. Good friends. Good food.

Maybe the fair's not the same anymore. But it's still the fair. I hope you don't miss it.

20

SUCH ARE THE DREAMS

When she was young, before she had formula stains on her clothes or crows' feet around her eyes or stretch marks, your mother had dreams. In those dreams, she was a singer or artist or engineer or a CEO. She wore designer clothes and her hair was always perfect and she always had a healthy bank balance—no one ever looked at her debit card with disdain. Her vacation plans never included fast food or Motel 6.

For many mothers, there was a man in those dreams. Strong, handsome, intelligent, and sensitive, he never left his dirty clothes on the bathroom floor, never left the seat up, and never forgot her birthday. Depending on whose dream it was, he liked to eat out a lot, never told her how to drive, and wasn't as scared of spiders as she was.

Sometimes there were children in the dreams, ones who behaved well and stayed clean and ate their vegetables without complaining. They did their homework and turned it in on time and never watched crummy television or listened to music that made her ears hurt. Even after she gave birth to these children (painlessly, with hair and makeup intact) she regained her figure instantly and never looked like death-warmed-over because her babies were the kind who slept through the night and whose teeth appeared miraculously straight and without pain.

Her home was a portrait of good taste and comfort. Its plumbing was never iffy, its windows never leaky, its floor never sloped with the passage of time. The furniture shone with the polish of quality and good wax. The beds were made each morning and the pillows arranged in the artful disarray that magazines make look easy. The mortgage, if there was one, was easily manageable. Robbing Peter to pay Paul was an unknown concept.

It is said that dreams die hard.

Not always. Sometimes, instead of dying, they just change—often for the better. We wear what is comfortable and affordable, we have bad hair days and...not so bad hair days, and time does leave its obvious and inexorable footprints across our skin. Most of our careers aren't glamorous, but if we're lucky, we still like them. They still pay the mortgage—which is probably less manageable that we'd hoped for—and keep the bank balance in the black. Not the very black, maybe, but close enough to keep the wolves from the door.

The men in our lives are different from what we dreamed, as faulty and fallible as we ourselves are. On any given day, they'll probably have some of the characteristics of the dream guys, but chances are good they'll never have them all at once.

Which brings us to the children of our dreams. Ahem.

If one of mine happened to be behaving well, the other two were not. They dressed okay, but were seldom clean at any time previous to their twelfth birthdays, at which time they suddenly started taking two showers a day and setting up housekeeping in front of the bathroom mirror. They did homework spasmodically and subsisted on diets that even now the memory of makes my stomach clench. They watched, read, and listened to every single thing I ever didn't want them to.

There was no single day during their growing-up years that

every bed in the house was made or every dish clean at the same time. The windows leaked, the plumbing required constant care and repair, and a few of the floors would have felt right at home under a ski lift. The surfaces of the furniture were marred by marks from compasses, baseball cleats, and the rubber soles of size 12 basketball shoes. And dust. Lots of dust. Because there would be time later to worry about those things.

I wrote this in the early 1990s, when our family of five had just started to expand. There are 16 of us now. Another generation of size 12 shoes, homework-at-their-convenience, and toilet seats always left in the wrong position. More dust.

When I was young, I had dreams. They've all come true. Every last one.

I hope yours have, too. Happy Mother's Day.

21

FATHER'S DAY

Webster defines a father as "the male parent of a child."

However, when one parent is absent, the parent who's doing the raising must fulfil both roles. Single mothers learn more about sports and changing oil and that time in their sons' lives when they become walking, talking hormones than they ever wanted to learn. Single fathers attend more dance recitals, buy more clothes with lace on them, and learn the hard way to keep their mouths shut when their daughters are "becoming women," since anything they say is going to be wrong anyway.

Father's Day, a very traditional day, isn't always that traditional anymore. Sometimes the fancy card goes to Mom instead of to Dad. Or to a stepfather, grandfather, or family friend. Everything is changing, but the things a father does still have to be done by someone.

Someone still has to play a thousand games of Horse under the basketball goal with the boy or girl who wants to be the first nine-year-old to play on the varsity team.

Someone has to chase the baseballs thrown or hit into the

nettles down by the fence and talk the monsters out from under the bed.

And say No and mean it.

Someone has to sit on the bleachers through all kinds of weather and pretend the wind, rain, and snow are no bother at all. Someone has to drop off. And pick up. Repeat.

Someone has to lie awake and worry when kids are late, because lying there worrying will surely keep them safe. It's part of the holding tight that someone must do. And the letting go.

Someone has to make the kid mow the yard and take out the trash and do the dishes even when it would be easier on the nerves and less time-consuming to just go ahead and do it and let the kid not learn about boring, day-to-day responsibilities.

Someone has to keep silent about hair that's too long and skirts that are too short and pants that look ridiculous. To clamp down on instinctive disapproval of ideas that seem wrong but are really only different and new, yet still know where to draw the line. When to speak up and describe in graphic, parental terms what is meant by decency, common sense, and respect for oneself and others. To reiterate that No means No and first and always Do No Harm.

Someone must show children the miracles of sunrise, sunset, and the grass growing quietly in the spring. They must sit on the back porch with these children and listen to the stories of their worlds gone wrong. And that person has to know when to jump in and fix it and when to stand aside and let them cope. And learn. And sometimes suffer.

Someone must, at all costs, do their best to keep them safe, to take the pain, fear, and pride that fatherhood brings and run with it.

There are a lot of these people around. Little League parks and bleachers are full of them. They can be found underneath the cars belonging to teenagers, being the push power behind the swings at the park, and standing at the mall with an open wallet and woebegone expression. They stand at the airport or carry too much stuff up too many steps to a dorm room when the kid leaps headlong out of the nest and wonder how it all happened so fast.

It's a long, hard job, but the rewards are boundless. Thanks to all who do it. Happy Father's Day.

22

FOR BETTER, FOR WORSE, FOR ALWAYS

"A successful marriage requires falling in love many times, always with the same person."
~~ Mignon McLaughlin

WHAT'S IT LIKE, you ask, being married to the same person for over 30 years? How do you do it?

Well, it's like this.

You know every word of his body language, can identify every freckle that dances across his shoulders when he walks into the sun, can buy him a year's wardrobe in 15 minutes flat counting the time you spend writing the check and asking the store clerk how her kids are doing. You know better than to cook tuna casserole even if you like it, that a sure way to get him to talk to you is to start reading a book, that if you're not feeling well, he's most certainly feeling worse.

You've learned by now that there's no possible way you can be in love every day.

Sometimes, let's come right out and say it, he's just a jerk. Sometimes, since we're not holding back, you're a pain in the neck. On those days, you look at each other with glazed eyes and wonder which lawyer to call. Then you go to bed, mumble "I love you" with doubtful sincerity, and lie in the dark and mentally parcel out the furniture, the dishes, and the retirement accounts until sleep overtakes you.

There are days, indeed, when Peggy Lee's voice echoes in your mind, *Is that all there is?* In the time when you had a flat stomach and naturally glowing skin and hair that was... well, a different color than it is now, this isn't what you counted on, was it? Once you got the kids raised, you were going to travel, wear expensive clothes, dance the night away. You were going to have *fun*.

Okay, you say, if it's that bad, why do you stay married?

Well, because, that's why.

Because he can tell by the set of your chin if you've had a bad day, because he'll bring home takeout food just when you're positive you can't cook one more meal in this lifetime, because he tells you he thinks you're really cute and means it even if you're not wearing any makeup and you haven't sucked your stomach in.

He still takes the street side on sidewalks because that's the way he was taught, tells your daughter she's *almost* as pretty as you are, and never reminds you you're getting more like your mother every day. He knows the words to the same songs you do and he doesn't mind that you can't carry a tune in a bushel basket. He doesn't laugh when you can't finish singing *Puff, the Magic Dragon* because you are in tears you can't explain. He just tucks his arm around you and hands you a tissue and kisses the top of your head where the roots are starting to show a bit.

Well, fine, you say, but isn't it boring?

Oh, I suppose, once in a while.

But a long marriage is like the sun. It's there every day and night, sometimes hidden by dense and sulky cloud covers, sometimes blazing red and vital and exciting. During cold spaces in your life—and life offers a lot of those—marriage wraps itself around you and keeps you warm.

The other side of that is that long marriages are uncomfortable now and then, like when you and your spouse disagree on matters of fundamental importance, such as values, religion, politics, money, and thermostat settings. And you do disagree about these things even though you think you never will. This is when you look at him and think, Why am I still married to this person who is so wrong about everything?

Maybe because, when you get right down to it, the marriage isn't boring, but a definition of *fun* you never imagined. And then there's the irrefutable fact that when the world is out to get you, it has to go through him first. Or, trite as it sounds, perhaps it's glued by those promises you made when he was just safely home from Vietnam and you were a size five, the ones about loving and cherishing and sickness and health...you know the ones I mean.

Or maybe because, like the sun, marriage is different most every day. Those differences are what have landscape painters and photographers lying in wait for sunrise and sunset. Some days they go inside in disappointment because the cloud cover hangs low and dismal over the show, but on other mornings and evenings they sit spellbound and work as fast as they can, holding onto the light for every precious second.

And there you go. There's the answer to the questions, What's it like, being married to the same person for over 30 years? How do you do it?

You just hold onto the light.

23

FREE

I like money. I used to like working with it in my job. I liked paying bills and working out the best way to do it so that we'd have as much money as we had last month—well, most of the time. Having more of it would be nice, I guess, but since we don't really *need* more, that doesn't really matter. I like what money *can* do, but not what it often *does* do.

Even though I like it, I don't want it to become important. At least, I don't want it to become more important than things that are free. When I wrote that, I thought it was sort of profound. I also thought some people reading it would just think it was goofy. And I'm good with that.

But this afternoon on Facebook, I saw pictures of some of our kids and grandkids on different beaches. The sky and the waters of Lake Michigan and the Atlantic Ocean were brilliant blue behind them. The sand was sparkling white. Another of the kids told me about a bicycle ride down the Virginia Creeper Trail. Seventeen miles almost all down-hill. I'm not sure I'll ever make the ride, but it's been fun thinking about it, visualizing our son and daughter-in-law riding it, remembering the conversation.

Oh, yes, conversation. Conversation with friends and family

is free and priceless at the same time. And sometimes it doesn't have to be friends or family. In 1973, I waited in line at Disney World behind a couple from Massachusetts who had moved to Georgia. Their accents were a hilarious mash-up, and I still remember the conversation.

Ditch lilies. I like lilies anyway—they're pretty. We have a yellow day lily that blooms like sunshine day after day. But those orange ones in the ditches all over the place—they light up everything, especially when they're sharing space with a rainbow of other wildflowers.

Speaking of lighting up, the Big Dipper and all those other star formations (I only know two, so I'm not going to try to sound smart here) give a free light show every night the clouds don't cover them up. The moon is another extravaganza that doesn't have a cover charge and is worth a crick in your neck to watch in every presentation from full to the slender quarter known as God's Thumbnail. Sunrises and sunsets are amazing and awesome. Although I think both those words are overused, they're also fitting at every dawn and every dusk.

Jokes are free and funny and good for you because they make you laugh. The more laughter you use, the more you want to use, and it never runs out. It's not fattening, either.

Music is a balm to the spirit. I think live music is best, and it's easy to find a place to go and listen. But when I look back to the endless years of my adolescence, I'm pretty sure the only reason I survived was that it was the Sixties and I got to listen to the best music ever on WLS and WABC (at night when it came in on the radio) and WOWO.

No one charges you for crying when you're sad, and sometimes tears are the best salve for emotional pain.

If you are able, nothing is better exercise than walking. Reading is endless entertainment. Watching a bird and a squirrel have a conversation, kids playing baseball, or babies laughing out loud can be day-makers.

Beauty is free. Artists in galleries are always happy to see you come in. To show you the pieces of their hearts that are on display there. To explain the things about art that you might not understand. The feelings you get in those places don't have a price on them. They are like music only you can hear.

Libraries are windows on the world—yes, I know that's not an original thought. I admit a lot of people have to pay for cards, but the truth is there is no charge to use the resources inside the building and often the programs offered are free and open to all. These include movies, music, crafts, story-time, study rooms, and great discussion groups.

Kindness is free. Holding doors for people, smiling even if it makes your cheeks hurt because you don't feel like it, or going through the express lane with only as many purchases as the sign allows. Remembering, when a kid is screaming, that sometimes it's just hard being two, three, or four, and hard being the mom or dad, too. Calling and saying, "Are you okay? I miss you."

The smell of flowers. Of sheets fresh off the clothesline. Of new-plowed earth or just-cut grass or hay or the sweetness of a baby's neck. The sounds of birds. Of laughing. Of "hey, batter, batter…" Of "I love you, too"—always a good answer.

When I started this, I wasn't sure how I was going to make it long enough, and now I don't know how to stop. I just went to see my sister, took her a book, and shared sciatica stories. We hugged each other, said we loved each other. It was free.

So, yeah, I still like money, but once you get past the food, clothing, shelter, and health care, it's not nearly as important as the things it can't buy.

Have a great week. Hug somebody—it's free.

24

GOING BACK

Yeah, this needs a date stamp on it. I'm sorry for that, but what I said after that election in November of 2016, I still mean, so I hope you don't mind.

I'm bewildered.

There are many things I liked about the "good old days." Fifty-seven Chevys, 60s music, bell-bottoms—yes, really, I did; using complete sentences that didn't include the f-bomb, not having to pump my own gas, milk in glass bottles, not knowing virtually everything good was bad for you. I could go on. And on. But then I remember other things, too.

My husband recalls black people having separate drinking fountains. The signs in Louisville used to say "colored," and he always wanted try it out to see if their water really was a different color.

He remembers coming home from Vietnam, when people turned away from him in his uniform. When the personnel director where he had worked before he was drafted didn't want to give his job back.

I remember not being able to get credit because of my gender and even when the bank finally gave me a loan in my own name, they sent the invoice for it to my husband.

I remember the day four little girls died in a church, the day James Meredith matriculated at the University of Mississippi, the day little Ruby Bridges was escorted into school by four federal marshals.

I remember that there were no girls' sports when I went to school, that we all had to wear dresses no matter how cold it was, that pregnant girls couldn't attend school but the boys who helped create the condition not only went to school but participated in extracurricular activities as if they were still fresh-faced virgins.

So, no, I'd just as soon not go back to the good old days. The good parts remain fresh in my memory (unlike what I came into the room for or my own name) and the bad parts are…

Well, they're back, is what they are. Meanness and lies and racism and misogyny and homophobia and a few other isms and phobias have taken us over. We are all—from both sides of the tall, ugly political fence—shocked that people we've known all our lives actually *aren't* people we've known all our lives.

The day after the election, I posted a quote from Lincoln's First Inaugural address on Facebook. It went like this: "We are not enemies, but friends. We must not be enemies. Though passion may have strained it must not break our bonds of affection. The mystic chords of memory, stretching from every battlefield and patriot grave to every living heart and hearthstone all over this broad land, will yet swell the chorus of the Union, when again touched, as surely they will be, by the better angels of our nature."

My son said, "Mom, forty days later, Confederates fired on Fort Sumter."

So there it is. Some of my favorite quotes—indeed, some of the *best* quotes ever anywhere, came from Abraham Lincoln. Other than a few Southerners I've met who are still fighting the

"War of Northern Aggression," I don't know anyone who disagrees with that. One of my favorite movies is *Gettysburg*, with its heartrending music and the scene on Little Roundtop that wears me out as much as if I'd been there. The movie of *Lincoln*, with Daniel Day-Lewis playing the president made me cry over the devastation and the glory of his life.

But how awful the good old days of Lincoln were. A war where 620 million Americans died. A culture that said it was okay for people to own other people. Native Americans being pushed farther and farther from their own land. Women's rights were laughed at, children didn't have any, and if anyone was of a different sexual persuasion than white heterosexual, well, woe be upon them.

So we went forward. Of course, we did, and along with the scars always left on a country's landscape by war, we ended up with wonderful quotes and accomplishments from those who led then.

But we didn't learn, did we? It's been over 150 years and we didn't learn. Although we have good memories, good accomplishments, and great quotes from a multitude of Americans, we are more divided than most of us have ever seen. We are angry and scared and we don't trust each other. What we thought we knew, we didn't know at all.

Because we went back.

When I first started this column, I started with two words, then I couldn't figure out where to go with them. How to explain. I still can't.

I'm still bewildered.

25

HITTING THE PAUSE BUTTON

"Some people hate funerals. I find them comforting. They hit the Pause button on life and remind us that it has an end. Every eulogy reminds me to deepen my dash, that place on the tombstone between our birth and our death."
~~ *Regina Brett*

UNLIKE THE PERSON I've quoted above, I do hate funerals. My faith tells me they are celebrations of beginnings, but the truth is they still feel like endings to me. That being said, I think things are different now—we laugh during funerals without trying to hide it, because the memories people leave behind are often both precious and funny; we really do celebrate the lives of those we've lost.

Do you ever wonder what people will think and say about you after you've died? I never did, either, until today.

My aunt died this week at 97. She'd lived a full and happy life, working outside the home and remaining childless during a time when those just weren't the things to do. She loved and cherished her husband, but after he died, she carried on for over 30 years without him.

Today was her funeral, and the minister who officiated there had never met her. She wasn't a churchgoer, and since she came from out of state, the man who spoke the usual words of comfort and parting was a stranger both to her and to most of us who attended. I thought he did a great job. But the one who did the best job was the one who signed the card accompanying a floral arrangement with the words, "For the best friend I ever had."

On the way home from the cemetery, while the mud dried on my high heels and I tried to keep the hem of my dress coat off the not-very-clean floor of my car, I thought about those words. And, since I've spent the last 24 years of my life, since the day my first child was born, feeling either guilty or worried or both, I got worried about the whole situation.

Would my sons remember that I drove them to at least 10,000 games and practices or would they remember that sometimes I yelled at them because I was just too tired to cope one more minute?

Would my daughter remember all the fun we had shopping and talking and being together or would she only recall the times I'd grounded her "for life, not one minute less"?

Would they remember the movies I took them to or the ones I didn't?

Would my husband mourn me forever, which I wouldn't want him to do, or forget me in the space of time it took him to learn how to buy his own socks, which I wouldn't want him to do, either?

Would my mother-in-law remember how much I loved her or would she remember my hit and miss (mostly miss) housekeeping, so opposite of hers?

Would people say, "she tried hard," or would they say, "she never could get anything quite right"?

Fortunately, it's only about six miles from the cemetery to my house, so that was all the time I had for worrying about things like that. But I thought about them all evening, as I thought about my aunt. I thought about the eulogies I've heard—both the ones that moved me to tears and the ones that left me cold and wondering who or what on earth the officiant was talking about.

It's nothing you can control. You just do the best you can and hope it's enough. You don't, or at least you shouldn't, worry about things like the ones I fretted about today in the car. You should worry about what you do while you're alive.

And if you have a best friend, maybe you should send them some flowers or a card and tell them how you feel about them. Soon. Because while it was a lovely eulogy to my aunt, they are words that should be spoken among the living, too.

26
IF WE JUST DO THIS...

*L*et's talk about my bathroom.

It's a half-bath with a window and good lights over the sink. You can't change clothes in there—no room. Years ago, one of our grandsons claimed it as his bathroom because it was little like him. He said the big bathroom was mine but that I had to let Papaw use it.

This bathroom has a good mirror. It's where I put on makeup, dry my hair, and count the lines multiplying on my face on a daily basis. I turn my head from side-to-side trying to determine just how many chins I have and if they're sagging more today than they did yesterday. I brush my teeth there, giving the mirror a captivating arrangement of white spots on its surface.

The top of the vanity is always a mess. When I clean the sink, I put stuff away, but by the next day it's all out again. I need to clean the sink more often.

I watch the deer from the little bathroom window. On occasion, I go into the little room and close the door. Then I lean on the windowsill and cry over one thing or another. (This would be a good time to tell me I'm not the only person who cries in the bathroom.)

But I digress.

My bathroom needed a new commode. A taller one that flushed on demand and didn't run for hours at a time if no one noticed. It has needed it for a while, but there's no need to talk about that—when you're in retirement, you put things off. Because you can. And because you have the other bathroom you can use. The big one. (Yeah, I know I said there was no need to talk about that, but it's one of those arguments I lost, so maybe I just needed to get it out of my system. Thank you for listening.)

But we bought a nice new commode. I thought, since we were going to put that in, I'd rip off the wallpaper and repaint while we were at it. And we needed a new window, too. The one that was there had leaked at some point, so we needed to check out that wall once I got the paper off. Oh, dear.

So we tore out that wall. Because we needed to move the vanity to gain access to the wall, we took it out, too, being careful because all I needed in the bathroom was a new toilet. And paint. And a window. And a wall.

Since the vanity was out, we thought we may as well replace the flooring. We have plenty of really nice wood laminate left over from my office. But my oak vanity will look terrible with it. Plus I hate that sink and the faucet is old and kind of ugly.

Okay, a new vanity. And sink. And faucet. And wall. And floor.

Did I mention that the medicine cabinet, the light bar, and the storage cabinet are also oak? Not to mention the towel rack, the toilet paper holder, and the switch- and receptacle-plates. The new vanity I chose after spending hours and hours looking is gray. Oak won't work.

Maybe I could paint... no, probably not. So I bought a new mirror to go with the vanity, and am going to spend hours and hours looking for a new light bar. And a towel bar, toilet paper holder, and switch plates. Maybe a storage cabinet, too. And a wall. And a floor. And...

We'll need new trim around the door, and since we can no longer match any of the boards around the floor or the window, we'll need to get that, too.

I want some new towels. And curtains for the very nice new window. Pretty soon, my bathroom will be done. It'll be so nice and we'll be glad we did it. Soon.

But then we want to take the tub out of the big bathroom and put a new shower in that space. We have an oak vanity, light bar, medicine cabinet, and storage cabinet in there, too. The windows and walls are good, but we need a new hamper. And towels. And maybe new towel bars—ours are really dated. Hmm…

But no, there's no need to talk about that.

27

NOT SO SELF ASSURED...

One of my least attractive qualities is my singing voice; therefore, it is a public service that I only sing in the car when I'm alone or at church when I can't help myself. So today, driving up 100 West alone on the way to Rochester, I was yelling singing along with the Beatles. The song was "Help," a favorite I hadn't heard for a while. It wasn't one I'd ever thought that much about. But we're approaching year's, time to choose my word for the one coming up0, and I think "help" might be the one.

We all need it sometimes.

We all need to give it sometimes.

We don't always recognize it at the time we receive it.

We occasionally resent the ones who are trying to help us.

Now and then we resent the ones who need help.

If we do it for thanks or recognition, we're doing it for ourselves, not for the recipient. (This is hard for me—I *love* recognition.) If we're doing it to get paid, it's still help, but it's also self-serving; I think maybe that dilutes it.

There are complications with the word. If you are asked for help and you really don't have time for it, you need to say no. But does that make you a terrible person? No, it means you've been overwhelmed often enough that you're finally on your way to finding the time to take care of yourself. It's kind of like the oxygen mask on the plane that you have to put on yourself before you put one on your child—if you don't have yours on, you can't save him or her. Sometimes you have to put on the mask and say no.

The other side of that complication is being able to accept help. Gracefully. If you happen to be "of a certain age" and your joints don't hurt and you can get up from the floor after you've foolishly gotten down there and you can still heft bags of salt and five-gallon bottles of water without even flinching... well, that's really good. I don't believe you, but that's good. However, if someone offers to help with things that are heavy or too difficult, say "yes, please," and, when they're done, give them cookies and say "thank you" again.

If you need a ride because driving's become an issue, accept one from someone else. If you have to, ask for one. Remember that in earlier days you were the one who gave rides. It's called paying it forward. My neighbor was always so grateful when I took her somewhere, although she took me plenty of places, too. Her funeral was this week, and I'd give a lot to be able to give her another ride.

There are times when the only help a person needs is for you to listen to him or her. To laugh at his jokes even if you've heard them before, to ask for a recipe even if you're probably never going to use it.

Helping, I have heard, is the same thing as enabling. If you give things, people won't want to earn those things on their own. If you donate money, chances are it won't be used in the way you intended. If you buy Christmas gifts for kids in need, their parents will just feel free to spend their money on things like drugs and tobacco and liquor.

Yeah. Sometimes. So? Does that mean you should let people be hungry, be without basic needs, that children shouldn't have

Christmas presents because their parents might be losers? Or does it just mean you should help anyway?

It's getting uncomfortable up here on my soapbox of righteousness. In case I make it sound like I always do the right thing, I don't. If I make it sound like I have all the answers, I don't. If I always, at my Pollyanna worst, make everything sound easy, it's not.

But that doesn't mean we shouldn't all try.

Have a great week. I hope you help someone. If you need help, I hope you get what you need.

28

IMPORTANT PLACES

My father-in-law was here this morning for a while. Seeing him, naturally enough, made me think about my mother-in-law, and miss her. And my mom—and miss her, too. I gave him a cup of coffee and thought about how many cups of coffee there had been at how many tables and then I thought of places that have been important to me.

In case you didn't know it, this is how a writer's mind works. Forget any idea of sense or linearity or neatly dovetailing thoughts—there aren't any of those. A writer's mind is a whole lot like the junk drawer at the end of the cabinet, full and messy.

But, yes, places. Starting with kitchen tables. My mother's, where the homemade bread and sugar cookies cooled and she taught me to iron pillowcases. My sister's, where no one was ever a stranger. My mother-in-law's, where we sat while she cooked and gave the grandkids whatever they asked for. The tables from our 30s where girlfriends and I sat and shared coffee and confidences. Our kitchen island now, where we play Farkle and I write Christmas cards and make plans. Kitchen tables are so many things—pulpits, confessionals, meditation sites, places of both privacy and society. They are where we laugh and cry and make life-changing decisions. They are important.

Desks have been instrumental since the first day of first grade, when I learned the word "Look" and from there on couldn't be stopped from reading every written page that crossed my path. It was at a desk where I learned to love American history although I never got good at it and where I had to stay through several recesses because of talking in class. It was where I was sitting when an editor first called and said, "I want to buy your book."

Bleachers are way up there on my list. They are where I watched my kids grow up and learn things that might have been missed outside the arenas of sports, drama, and music. They're where I had my first experience with civil disobedience back in high school. When I was 19, I sat in the bleachers at the softball diamond in Maconaquah Park and tried to figure out what I was going to do next.

Church. Obviously, it's the accepted place to worship, but I believe you can worship anywhere. It's also where people are married, baptized, dedicated, and eulogized. It's where we have chili suppers, noodle suppers, sauerkraut suppers, and tenderloin suppers—and that's just in September and October; there are plenty more to be had throughout the year. It's where, if we're lucky, party affiliations and grudges are left outside the open-to-all doors. It is, when all else fails, a safe place.

Norris Lake, Tennessee is important because our family in its entirety spent Thanksgiving weekend there a few years ago. It was one of the best times I've ever had—it's also the last time we've all been in the same place at the same time. That could be bittersweet, but it's not—it's all sweet. Although it's important not to live in the past, keeping good memories in a pocket inside your heart is just as important.

The Nickel Plate Trail. I don't walk much these days, but it's still my favorite place when I do. I've done a lot of plotting there, spent quality time with family and friends, and remembered what a gift nature is.

The school up the road is important if for no other reason than there have been family members in it ever since it was built. It's where I have so many memory bank deposits I can't begin to keep track of them all.

There are so many others. Favorite vacation places, the side yard where the deer graze and the birds dive-bomb each other and the sun slips quietly and beautifully into the horizon, places I've voted, music that has been so stirring it created places of its own.

The pleasure in important places is that you don't have to go back to them to experience them. As faulty as memory becomes—and it does—happy times still live there. You may not be able to remember how to get back to the physical places that are important to you, but you'll remember how you felt there. You'll remember the perfect meal with 16 of you at the table and the day you were laughing so hard you were falling off the barstools in the kitchen and the taste of those sugar cookies that you've never once been able to emulate. And you'll know those places—and times—were important. Capture the joy.

29

IT'S ABOUT RESPECT

That's hardly an original idea. Most of us heard it growing up, many of us have said it as parents. Often. We've said it within our marriages (through gritted teeth sometimes, which is quite a trick but can be done), about the flag, and about the national anthem. About teachers and preachers and law enforcement officers and people in the military—past and present.

I've always thought it was pretty easy to be respectful. Even if you have biases—and we all do, whether we like admitting it or not—keeping them to yourself is a good thought. They're a kind of poison, and if you spread them around, you're spreading toxicity. It's that spreading that teaches kids about hate, because they're not born knowing it. I'm not trying to say it's okay to have them as long as you don't hurt anyone with them, but I am saying it's better.

It's also easy to be respectful of people you agree with, or ones who look like you or worship like you do or love like you do or never need anything from you. It's easy when respect is part of a bandwagon thing where one finds safety in numbers. Although my ideology doesn't entirely fit at church, I am nevertheless always safe there. Our likenesses are bigger and, I believe that in our hearts, they are more important than our differences.

But then come the times when you absolutely can't deal with what someone else believes. Thinks. Does. How they live. When you wake up to the discovery that people you've known all your life aren't who you thought they were. When they discover the same thing about you.

That's where the choices come in. The ones that we all have. We can turn our backs on those who've shocked or disappointed us. We unfriend them on Facebook, call them terrible names, spread things about them that may or may not be true—but just in case they are, the rest of the world needs to warned—or just disappear from their lives leaving them wondering where we went. Or why.

Or we can bite down hard on our bottom lips and remember why we had those people in our lives in the first place. Because those reasons are still there. No matter who they voted for, they're still the person who's had your back since you were in study hall together. No matter where they worship—or don't—they're the ones you've sat shoulder-to-shoulder with and laughed until you cried. No matter how you feel about their life choices, they weren't choices for you to make. No matter what their lifestyle is, you're not required to live it; if you're their friend, your job is to support them.

A caveat here—I know this won't work all the time. I know turning your other cheek is finite even if it's not supposed to be. I know some of the things we learn about others are gaspers that make us lie in the dark and wonder how we can look at them again knowing what we know now.

It's hard. Really hard. And I understand, regardless of my Pollyanna tendencies, that acceptance isn't always the right answer; sometimes you have to stand up. But you can do it without calling names—even if they did it first—because a never-ending truth is that you can't unsay things. You can't unhear what others have said. You don't have to agree with others' opinions—that's why they're opinions—but you need to defend their right to have them.

You don't have to like anything about the way they live, but as long as they're not hurting anyone, it doesn't really have anything to do with you. I've read that "what other people think of you is not your business" (I think Deepak Chopra said it, but there were a slew of attributions) and even though I think it's a painful thought, it's also true. What you think of them, however, is your business.

Find the good, remember the reason you had them in your life, laugh at the memories. Grit your teeth and keep on scrolling. If you can't like them anymore, just remember when you did. Also remember when you're standing up is that the other person is, too.

Now that I've written this, I'm hearing Aretha Franklin in my head and am sitting here singing R-E-S-P-E-C-T (badly), so I looked at the lyrics to see if there were some that would fit into the end of this column. I didn't think that was going to work, until I got to this one line: "Keep on tryin' (just a little bit)…"

I will. I hope you do, too.

30

IT'S IN THE MAIL...

At a writers' group meeting, Pam, one of the other writers who has a writing voice so deep and poetic I cringe with envy every time she writes, said she'd been writing letters. "Oh," I said, "it's a lost art." And I realized that whether it was a lost art or not, *I'd* certainly lost it.

I blogged about it, using some of the same words I'm using here. That's what you do in letters—you tell the same news to everyone you write to. *We lost a tree last week in that wind. A new cat has shown up at the bowl on the porch. We don't need another cat, but he's so pretty. We got an inch of rain last night—slept right through it. The kids are growing up too fast. Why did I ever say I couldn't wait to see what they'd be like when they were older? I could have waited. Did you hear about my cousin passing away? So many memories. I should have gone to see her, but never got around to it. Went by your folks' old house and someone painted it pink—wouldn't your dad have a fit?*

They weren't important, those letters, that news. Yet they were. Remember opening envelopes and having school pictures drop out? Sometimes a check. Sometimes a five-dollar-bill you needed more than you could bear thinking about. My mom and aunt were the queens of sending clippings. Obituaries, jokes, quotations. We found them in their Bibles after they passed away, with dates written at the tops in faded ink. Oh, yes, memories.

I worked at the post office for 30 years, watching the amount of personal mail drop almost on a weekly basis. There were still lots of greeting cards, especially at Christmas, Mother's Day, and Valentine's Day, but not so many letters addressed to colleges, military installations, nursing homes and senior living complexes. It was a sad lessening, a step away from an important way of communicating.

My friend Judith and I still exchange letters three or four times a year. We used to meet for lunch, and I miss that, but in all honesty, I would miss the letters more. If she reads this, I hope she realizes she owes me one. Or maybe she doesn't...but if she thinks she does... *Dear Judith. It's rough getting old sometimes, isn't it?*

I used to have pen pals, didn't you? And I wrote to school friends in the summer because country kids didn't see the others from May until September except for 4-H meetings and church. To other school friends who moved away but are still friends all these many years later. I wrote to my aunt and my grandma and to siblings if they were living far away.

I wrote thank-you notes, because my mom insisted on it, and I'm glad I learned how. I must admit, I never got good at it. *Dear Grandma and Grandpa. Thank you for the money. Love, Liz.*

When my boyfriend was in Vietnam, I wrote to him. All these years later, I still call him the Boyfriend and I write him notes sometimes. He reads them and puts them away in his dresser drawer. He doesn't write notes to me, but is the master of choosing just the right card for any occasion or, better yet, any non-occasion. *Dear Duane. I'll be so glad when you get home.*

I have my parents' letters to each other, written before they married. I wish I could have known the people they were then, seen the relationship they shared, felt the love they had for each other. It was different by the time I came along. They'd lost a beloved child and, I think, too much of themselves to ever recover the young and hopeful people they had been. There used to be more than one mail delivery a day, and Mom and Dad took advantage of that tenuous connection between Elkhart and Gilead. *Hey, there, nice kid. How's your day?*

I've read some of John and Abigail Adams' letters. I love how he began letters to her—"My dearest Friend..." What better thing is there to be than someone's dearest friend? *I desire you would remember the ladies...*

Every now and then someone sends me a handmade card with a note in it. It's such a great gift to get. Local artists sell greeting cards with prints of their creations on the front. They're beautiful, and when you send one, someone will put it on their fridge or their mantel or the table beside the bed. They'll think of you. They'll smile. Their hearts will be lighter.

Letters are dreams on paper, aren't they? They're memories and information and secrets and cherished conversations you can read again and again and again. They're stories that might never have been told if someone hadn't addressed a letter. They are precious things.

I hope you're having a wonderful day and that you'll write and tell someone about it. They'll be so glad to hear from you.

31

IT'S TODAY

*D*o you have days you look forward to...more than others, I mean?

My husband, the roommate, sits in wait from the day after Christmas until February first. Because then the longest, darkest month with the shortest, coldest days is over. Theoretically. According to *his* theory, that is. Because I know, of course, that Punxsutawney Phil is going to stick his head out the next day and haul it back inside rather than freeze to death in the darkness of his shadow.

When I was a kid, I looked forward to Valentine's Day because everybody in the class gave nearly everyone else a valentine. And we got candy. Then I looked forward to Easter because there was often a new dress in it for me, not to mention we wore new white shoes to church instead of the black patent ones that hadn't survived the ravages of winter all that well. We had ham for Sunday dinner, the grandparents came to visit. And we got candy.

There were other days of excitement. I loved the Fourth of July, complete with a parade and fireworks and unlimited hot dogs. And candy. The first day of school, complete with new clothes and new books (yes, even then I had a thing for books) was a biggie all the way from the first year to the last. Getting out of school for the summer, when hot days were so new and delicious. Thanksgiving and Christmas were my favorite can't-waits.

When the kids were little, especially for a few periods when I had two in diapers, I couldn't wait until they were housebroken. Until they could talk. Until they went to school. Until the miserable years of junior high had passed. Until they graduated.

I wrote... oh, always. I wanted to write a column so much, couldn't wait to see my byline wherever it appeared. I wanted to write a book, and couldn't wait for the box of author copies, the first book-signing (I practiced my signature. Seriously.), and the first check.

I'm not sure when it all changed. When I stopped saying, "Oh, I can't wait..." about times, events, things. When my emotional February first became unimportant because all the days before it were so much fun and so full of life going on. It may have been when my firstborn reached six and a half feet and I wasn't sure how it happened, or when the roommate and I were celebrating our 25th wedding anniversary when... hey, wait, aren't *we* only 25?

It may have been while standing in a funeral home at someone's celebration of life regretting that there'd never been enough time together, enough laughing, enough comparing of life's notes, and laughing some more. Never enough.

No, I'm not sure when, but at some point, it all became about the journey. I still love holidays, but getting ready for them is more exciting than the actual days. I love my adult kids and grandkids, but I'm sorry if I wished away even one day of their growing up. I love having a new book, but the anticipation is more fun to me than Release Day, when my stomach hurts and I'm afraid no one will read it.

I still love writing this column, no matter how many starts and stops it's had over the years, but while I still look forward to that byline, I don't spend time thinking about it. There are too many other things to think about. To do. To laugh at. I can wait.

32
LET IT GO

The title of this post is the name of a perfectly lovely song that has been over-played, over-exposed, and over-everything else. It's also the phrase Duane has used to me—several times—when I complained about changing times (and other things, but those can be my secret.) I despise the time change. I don't care whether we're on Eastern, Central, or Southwest Lilliputian time, just leave it alone! My husband, on the other hand, doesn't mind the time change nearly as much as he minds the fact that I just won't let it go.

Which leads me to other things.

- Bad reviews
- Weather
- The other side of the political aisle
- The church across town whose doctrine and signs drive you nuts
- Death and...
- ...taxes

These in turn lead me to different other things.

- The card you forgot to send
- The apology you've owed for years
- The bags in the laundry room that need to go to recycling, Goodwill, and the women's shelter
- Saying "I love you" and "you are so cool" and "I want to help" and "I'm so sorry this has happened to you" to those who need to hear it
- The laugh out loud and...
- ...a hug

The first list is, you got it, of things you should let go. So...just do. We'll wait over here in the corner while you go into the bathroom and scream really loud if that's what it takes.

The other list is, you got it, too!—of things you shouldn't let go. Of things it's never too late to do.

How about you? Do you have lists of your own? Go ahead and take care of them, then go out and have the best week ever—who cares what time it is?

33

LET'S BE THE HELPERS

*I*n 1918, my grandparents' oldest daughter, Amy, died in the influenza epidemic. She was 23. My grandmother used to spend a lot of time alone in her rose garden. Not until I had children of my own did I wonder if that was where she did her grieving.

In 1941, my parents second child, Christine, died of diphtheria. She was three. My sister still remembers the quarantine and that people stood outside at the funeral. Mostly she remembers growing up without her little sister. And that our parents were never the same again.

In 1948—71 years ago this week—my friend Debby's parents lost their first child, Janice, to polio. She was six. I remember Deb telling me about her mother talking to an elderly cousin when they were visiting a funeral home years later. They talked a lot, and it was a joy to Deb's mom to talk to someone about Janny. Someone else who remembered her.

When I was looking up dates for this, I saw that my great-grandparents lost a daughter when she was 14. Later, the two-year-old son of a great-uncle died and his father died two years later.

Loss. Grief. Irreversible life changes.

This, then, is what we fear the most, isn't it? These are the things that either break us or bend us so far there's no coming back to what we were. They remind us to be grateful for every day, because tomorrow's not promised. They also remind us not to give up, because if we do have those tomorrows, we need to make something of them, even if it's no more than the proverbial lemonade.

So here we are, in the middle of…something. It's different, I suppose, from those things I listed above, different even from 9/11. Because it's now, not then. We're learning some things on this tortuous path. How to enjoy our own company. How to refrain from physical contact. How to differentiate between want and need. How to take our time. We are reminded to cherish friends and family and connection.

There are hard lessons in this, too. That there are many, many people who don't care about anyone else. They are the ones who fill their grocery carts with staple items and too bad for everyone following them.

That there are many, many people who continue to play the blame game for the situation even when it's obvious there are no winners. Democrats versus Republicans, Liberals versus Conservatives, Millennials versus Boomers. I am guilty of this, too—not of blaming anyone for the virus itself but of blaming officials for their responses (or lack thereof) to it. So, I repeat, to you and me alike, there are no winners in the blame game. And again in case we didn't catch it the first two times, there are no winners.

We learn again what we really always knew, that different people prioritize different things. I've always rather scorned people who collect money just to collect it and because it's a way of keeping it away from someone else. Now I'm scorning people who collect toilet paper, bottled water, and ammunition the same way.

Volunteerism, always a backbone of society, is showing its strength during this crisis. Hands-up and hearts-out people are taking food to ones who can't get out and making sure children have meals even if they're not in school. Mr. Rogers' mother told him, "Look for the helpers" when things were scary. She was right. Let us not only look for them, but be them as well.

We are in large part remembering to be grateful to the essential personnel who are still working, who are taking care of the rest of us, often at risk to themselves. I can't help but wonder how long it will be before certain ones among us will once again be insisting they have no need to make a living wage for the work they do.

Columnist Connie Schultz says, "When this pandemic comes to an end, we will not be who we were at its beginning."

She's right, isn't she? I'd love to think we'll come out of it stronger and better and kinder. I'm going to try to do just that. Think that way and be that way, too. I hope we all will.

Have a great week. Be nice to somebody.

34

LIFE IN LAYERS

I am a writer. I write this column, I blog, I write books. All those things are different, but at the heart of it, I'm a storyteller. I try to tell the stories in layers, so that the story's residents are people and animals you care about and the events are ones you believe. When you reach the end, I hope you sigh with pleasure because you feel like you've been there.

So this evening I was thinking—I do this (or say I am) when the words aren't coming and I've only written like 12 of them in the last hour—about where those layers come from.

From the past. My grandparents had a fire in the big brick house where they lived. My grandmother, skinny as a rail except for her advanced stage of pregnancy, picked up the treadle sewing machine and carried it downstairs and outside. I don't know what else they lost, but no one was hurt and Grandma had her sewing machine. This was over 100 years ago, but the story hasn't changed by so much as a syllable in my lifetime. I don't know how she did it—I have one of those treadle machines and I can barely move it to clean under it—but she did. At least, so the story goes, and I'm not going to argue with it at this point.

I model my book heroines on that one incident. The women I

write about will never be extraordinary in looks or intelligence or accomplishment, but if life demands it, they will be able to carry the sewing machine down the steps. I know people like that, too—we all do. My friend Debby Myers' sewing machine is MS, and she carries its weight down the stairs every day. I know people with Stage Four cancer who live every single day as fully as we all should. They are most certainly tired and often ill, but they are alive, too. Courageously so.

From experience. If not our own, ones that are close to us. An accident happened in my Lake Minagua series of books, and entire families' lives are changed forever. Accidents much like the one I wrote about have happened locally. The community still feels the ripples. Friends and relatives still grieve. People still say, "…what if?"

From listening. My nephew and his wife have seven children between them, so when they go as a family, they usually take two cars. In December one year, they went to a family gathering several hours away. The three teenage girls rode with my nephew. He listened, laughed, learned, and was scared, and he knew all the girls better when they got there. I'm fairly certain he remained scared, but that's what parents do. It's only one of the layers you assemble when you raise people who mean more to you than life itself.

From airports. I don't know a single writer who doesn't love airports. We sit with our Starbucks cups and watch people and write their stories in our heads or even on our laptops if we haven't already run our batteries down. We hear accents and close our eyes to try and remember them. We feel the emotions of people saying Good-bye. Of others saying Hello.

From music. Although I write in silence, I hear music in my stories. I talk about songs and what they mean, the feelings they create. More layers. I see and write about people dancing in the kitchen, and that's the icing on top of that particular cake.

Layers are how we survive. Sometimes things are too painful

to take on all at once, so we do the Scarlett O'Hara thing and think about pieces and parts of them tomorrow. And the next day. Or maybe when we have someone to talk with—or to just listen while we talk. Some things make us so happy we want to stretch them out. There are occasional moments that frighten you with the intensity of their perfection. You have to put them in that place behind your heart and keep them safe until you need to bring them out and relive them. Layers again.

Have a great week. I hope your story has wonderful layers.

35

LITTLE BOXES

Sometimes, the workings of my mind make me think of that Parker Brothers game, Scattergories. I don't know how to play it—its bright red box isn't one of those taking up room on a shelf upstairs with Monopoly, Scrabble, and Candyland—but I just feel like I have a whole bunch of little boxes with something to say in each one but not enough to make a point with. Quite honestly, I think I'd write a better column if I could settle into Cards Against Humanity or something, but the Scattergories have taken me over, and this is what I've been thinking.

About gifts. In our yard, outside my office window, we have a clothesline. I like to hang sheets and towels out because I love the smell of the sun and the wind in them. However, the towels come out stiff and scratchy and Duane would rather sheets were soft instead of crisp, so I don't hang many clothes. Instead, the suet feeder hangs on the pole and the birds congregate there to eat and scold each other. The deer wander up under the clothesline and look at the window until I move, at which time they chase each other back into the cornfield. I am not outdoorsy by any means, but you can't live in the country without realizing what a gift the outdoors is.

About gas prices. They're ridiculous. Not that they're so high, because I guess the truth is most everything, except wages, has gone up exponentially over the years. No, not because of that, but because you can spend a quarter less a gallon in Peru than you do in Logansport. Until tomorrow, when you need to go to Kokomo to spend that quarter less. Surely someone knows what this game is and what its rules are, but apparently it's set up so the same people win every time. I wonder who they are.

About driving in the left lane when you're neither passing someone nor turning left. Please stop it. You're in everyone's way and you're annoying.

About Denver Days. They'll be next weekend, starting Thursday. Peru's Second Saturday is next weekend, too. No reason to cook or watch TV when so much food and live entertainment is easily available and so much fun!

About politics. You have no idea how difficult it is *not* to write about politics. You're welcome.

About spelling and grammar. Yes, they are important. My freshman English teacher told the story of the parent who complained about her daughter having to take three years of English in high school. "I had to take it, too," said the mother, "and it ain't never done me no good." I rest my case.

On the other side of the same coin, my son-in-law insists math is important, too. However, he is a math teacher—what does he know? Well, maybe more than I do. He understands the whole Order of Operations thing and has explained it to me more than once. I don't get it. Make sure that you do; it will be helpful.

About music. It is the universal language, transcending religion, politics, gender, race, and all other divisions either innate or created. I don't care at all what you like, nor do I expect you to care what I like. But the truth is if you're playing yours loud enough while we're both at the gas station that it shakes my car, that's just dumb.

About milk. It should cost more. I'm glad it doesn't, but it should.

About blue jays on suet feeders. They're obnoxious. And so much fun to watch. They remind me of junior high, when all of life is socially awkward and physically clumsy and puberty was a nightmare from where there was no turning back.

About writing. I'm going to be entering another decade here in a year or so. Should I give it up? Should I not? And then I think, hey, I'm not going to stop coloring my hair, so why should I stop writing?

About girlfriends. I think they should be assigned a family classification, like sister-of-the-heart or wine-and-whine-with-woman. I don't love my girlfriends more than my sister or sisters-in-law, but I probably love them as much.

About being grateful. I am. Every day of my life.

There you have it. The Scattergories episode of the Window Over the Sink. Cards Against Humanity would probably be more fun, but this is a family column. Have a great week.

36

NOT JUST A PRETTY FACE

My friend Nan and I were talking about weight the other day. Actually, she was probably talking about it and I was obsessing about it. Which I've been doing since I was in the seventh grade and was consistently bigger than Linda, who lived down the road. I'm fairly certain I still am.

I have lost the equivalent of several versions of myself over the years. Fifteen pounds for class reunion, 25 for our daughter's wedding, an enthralling 40-some the year I retired. A couple of years in the 80s, I lost weight to wear a two-piece swim suit in Florida; once it was to wear my favorite-ever black-and-white polka-dotted dress to our younger son's graduation.

I've gained it back. Usually plus some. Every time. I do not, as my friend suggested, accept myself as I am. But I also do not eat sensibly or exercise enough. I don't tell the truth about my weight on my driver's license and I cringe at every doctor's visit because there's always that stop in the hallway between the waiting room and the examination room.

In all honesty, I hate being the size I am. I want to be the size I was when I first thought I was overweight. I also want to be able to eat a whole can of Pringles on a daily basis. Those things, as you can imagine, don't go together. I can win against the Pringles by not buying them—but that doesn't fix the fact that I've never met a carb I don't like.

There are terms that go along with being heavy. Some of them are just what they are: overweight, heavy, obese, fat. Some are silly euphemisms: chubby, jolly, round. A few are kind: curvy, voluptuous, big-boned. Then there are the others, when someone says, "she has such a pretty face," or "she let herself go," or the even crueler "tub of lard."

Then there is the issue of clothes. Like any other big girl, I'd like for my clothes to make me look like the size six I'm not. This isn't going to happen, especially when people who create catalogs, commercials, and magazine advertising persist in having size-zero models wearing plus-size clothing. Kudos to the retailers who have gone to the dark side and given us glimpses of fashion realism.

I blame no one for the extra pounds I carry on my woefully small bones; I have earned every ounce of them myself. But, blame or not, virtually no one who is heavy wants to be. Although many of them—me included—could maintain a healthy weight if they could also maintain a reasonable amount of willpower, that's a much easier thing to say than it is to do.

Hopefully I will lose some on my next foray into eating right and I will weigh less and feel better and never gain it back. I wish this not only for myself but for everyone else who has a daily struggle with poor self-image. If you need to gain weight and can't, I hope a few pounds (preferably mine) come your way. If you have terrible hair, I hope you find the right cut or color or whatever it takes. If you don't like your teeth, find a dentist who deals not only in dental health but in smiles. If you just don't like what you see in the mirror, talk to someone who loves you; they have a much better view of you than you do.

On the days when you really can't make peace with how you

look, it's much more important to remember that your weight and whatever other physical things about yourself are not who you are. Acceptance is hard to come by when it comes to appearance, but that doesn't mean you can't like yourself. You can still laugh hard, love much, and make every day a good one.

37
DUST AND HUMMINGBIRDS AND BEING A SPECTATOR

Sometimes I think I should change the title of this column to "The Rocking Chair on the Porch," because I've discovered a disturbing part of aging I hadn't expected—although I should have.

All these years after I gave up sitting on bleachers, I've once again become a spectator.

I am envious of people my age who have not. You know who you are, those of you whose flower beds still look great and who plant gardens and run your vacuum cleaners before walking across the carpet makes you sneeze. I'll bet you dust, too, before someone writes "dust me" on the table with a snarky finger. No doubt you cook meals every day, sometimes more than one a day. Most unforgivable of all, you probably have good hair, too.

Another meaning of the word "spectator," however, is "observer." I like that much better, don't you? Probably because it doesn't make me think about dust, weeds, or other people's hair.

So, here are some observations. Tell me what you think. Better yet, tell me some of yours.

- Hummingbirds either like you or they don't. They

don't like me, but they hover around my friend Carolyn Moon as if she hung the...moon. I'm fairly convinced Carolyn drives all over the place stealing birds from the rest of us. But maybe I'm imagining things. Maybe they really don't like me.
- I always like the color green, but in the spring, it becomes my favorite. I bought a pair of green pants that absolutely nothing matches. I splash little pictures of shamrocks all over things I write and I gush about the grass and the trees and how lush and beautiful they are. Duane mows three times a week in spring and doesn't gush nearly as much as I do, but, hey, I'm the observer here.
- At this point in my life (the rocking chair stage, remember?) it takes 15 minutes to get from Monday morning to Friday night. I have no idea what happens to the days in between. If I do find them, I invariably have the wrong one because when you don't get up to go to work, it's not necessary to know what day it is, right?
- If I am early or on time to an appointment, the other half of the appointment isn't ready for me. If I'm late—or have the wrong day; see above paragraph—the person's standing there twisting her hair and looking at her watch and rolling her eyes. I may be overdramatizing that a bit, but can't you just see it?
- No matter what your job is, everyone on Facebook could do it better than you do. They'd also do it in less time for less money.
- A common question is, "Do you prefer coffee or tea?" I answer this differently depending on the time of day, when the truth is if someone else is paying for it or pouring it for me, I'll take either. Thank you.
- When lookups for the word "exculpate" spiked

23,000% with *Merriam-Webster* on July 24, 2019, I was one of them. I was pretty sure I knew what it meant, but "pretty sure" has gotten me into trouble before.
- I haven't gained weight or appreciable wrinkles in my feet, and pink nail polish with sparkly little flowers on the big toes makes me feel good.
- If you are a Millennial or a Gen-Xer, talking trash about Baby Boomers does not endear you to us. If you are a Boomer and act like the trash they are talking, who can blame them?
- Generalizing is hardly ever a good idea. See above paragraph.
- If you don't know whether it's true or not, keep it to yourself. Even better, look it up.
- Calling people names has never done a single positive thing for anyone.
- Growing up in the same house or even the same community as others doesn't mean you're necessarily going to agree on things. Anything. Ever.
- You don't have to be a Christian to know that Acts 20:35 is the way to go. (Hint. I'll just give you the last part: "It is more blessed to give than to receive.")
- Sometimes you need to get out of the chair and walk somewhere. Maybe in someone else's shoes.

That last one tells me I'm not ready to change the Window to a Rocking Chair. You're never too old to be productive, never too busy to be kind, never too poor to give. It's great to talk, but even better to listen—I'm talking to myself here, by the way—and laughing is the best thing of all.

38
OF GIFTS AND KEYS

I've been driving for mumble, mumble years. For months before I turned 16, I drove forward and backward the abbreviated length of our driveway so that if I learned nothing else, I had D and R figured out on the gearshift. I got my license, and never looked back. As much now as then, I love driving.

I admit traffic has lost whatever charm it may have had, and roundabouts are guaranteed to throw me into a panic attack on my third trip around them in search of my exit. The absence of turn signals—when did they remove them from cars?—and the preponderance of bright lights—heaven forfend you dim them when someone's coming from the other way; that's old school, right?—has made driving into a less-pleasant challenge. So has the slowing of my reflexes with age, the weird placing of Stop signs, and the fact that no one (myself included) always knows who goes first at an all-way stop.

So, 10 days or so ago, I had surgery. I'm doing great, feeling great, and have no complaints. Except that I can't drive. Well, actually, I could, but am under doctor's orders not to. Which means, I'm pretty sure, that if I snuck out from under my husband's watchful eye and drove... say, to church, which is less than 1000 feet away, and had a wreck, I'd be liable. So I'm not driving. Duane hasn't even had to hide the keys to my car.

And it's fine. Really it is. As I mentioned last night, he always wants to drive anyway. He said that had nothing to do with my surgery and there was no reason to write anything about that at all. What it has to do with is the fact that he hates my driving, but you didn't hear that from me.

To get back to the point, or at least close to it, even living in the country, I never realized how much a person's independence depended on driving. (I know that sentence is wrong, but I can't figure out why. If I hadn't already annoyed everyone I know by talking about being anesthesia-stupid, I would do it now.) I'm not what you'd call a social butterfly, but when I have to ask for a ride, I can be downright reclusive.

We have to figure our logistics down to the minute. He will drop me off at one place, go to do an errand, then pick me up and drop me off somewhere else. He'll be done before I am, so then he has to wait. I've heard that waiting is good for the soul, but personally, I don't think it's good for much, so I hate to ask someone else to do it. Especially someone who looked me straight in the eye the day after I had surgery and swore I absolutely did not look like crap on a cracker.

Actually, being humbled by having to ask for help isn't a bad thing, because we all reach a point when we can't do everything by ourselves. I don't lift bags of water softener salt anymore, and I'm not fond of the bottles that go into the water cooler—although they roll nicely if you just aren't up for lifting them. Carrying 27 bags of groceries into the house is no longer a one-trip option. Dusting is too labor-intensive. (Okay, I made that one up, but it works well there, doesn't it?)

Being unable to drive makes me think of what I hope is a long way down the road. The time will come when our kids will hold out their hands for the car keys because we will have become a risk to others on the road. It will be one of those "changing of the guard" events that occur in parent-child relationships. I imagine it will be a painful one for both sides. I hope I give in gracefully, but I'm not counting on it. I will undoubtedly remind them that I was the one who taught them to use a spoon. But then I'll give them the keys.

Yes, I'm missing the independence I get from driving, and, yes, I'll be glad to get it back. I think it's like most of the gifts in our lives in that we don't realize the finiteness of it until it stares us in the face. Let this be a reminder that we should, as with all those other gifts, enjoy it and take care of it while we have it. And when the time comes, we need to hand over the keys.

Have a good week. Be nice to somebody. Don't bother with dusting—it just comes back.

39
SMELLING THE ROSES...

I love being productive, when I can end a day tired but satisfied with what I've accomplished. When I look back at the days when the kids were all in school, my day looked something like this.

3:30 A.M.: Get up. Start washer and dryer, put away supper dishes, drink coffee, and get ready for work. Read a chapter of a book while folding the clothes that were in the dryer.

4:20 A.M.: Go to work. Trip takes 33 minutes. Allow extra seven minutes for emergencies such as flat tires, mountainous snow drifts, and having to stay in the car until "American Pie" stops playing on the radio or a chapter ends in an audio book.

5:00 A.M. – 1:30 P.M.: Work day job. Half hour lunch is long enough to return things to stores, pick up things at other stores, get caught by a train, and read another chapter while eating a hot dog from B & K.

1:30 P.M.: Go home from work. Trip often takes more than 33 minutes because other cars insist on using the road. Pick up things at the store I forgot to get at lunchtime.

2:05 P.M. – 4:15 P.M.: Put away the groceries I brought home. Reload washer and dryer and fold the clothes that were in the dryer. Drink coffee. Make the bed. Run the sweeper if the floor feels crunchy. Look at the can of Pledge in consternation, trying to remember why I bought it. Start supper, using mystery meat I defrosted in the microwave. Read a chapter while it's defrosting. Fall asleep and wake up when Duane comes home. Feel guilty because the house is never clean enough.

5:30 P.M.: Pick up first child at practice. Five-mile round trip.

5:50 P.M.: Pick up second child at practice. Five-mile round trip.

6:20 P.M.: Pick up third child at practice. Five-mile round trip.

6:30 P.M.: Explain to children that it would be much easier if they all came home at the same time. They could do their homework while waiting for the last practice to end. Glare back at the resultant blank looks.

6:35 P.M. – 7:30 P.M.: Eat supper, drop off assorted children for evening activities. Go home and fall asleep during *Jeopardy.*

8:00 P.M. – 10:00 P.M.: Dry and fold more clothes, do supper dishes, stuff Pledge can behind everything else so that I can never find it again, notice there's another Pledge can hidden in the same place. Shower and get ready for bed.

10:00 P.M. – 11:00 P.M.: Pick up children from wherever they've been dropped off, not getting out of the car because—didn't I mention I was ready for bed?

11:00 P.M.: Go to bed. Intend to read another chapter. Don't even get the book open. Regret never stopping to smell the roses everyone's always talking about.

(I must admit that Duane did some of the hauling of kids, but since this is my whine here, I felt perfectly fine leaving that part out.)

My schedule is much different in retirement.

Somewhere between 5:30 a.m. and 7:30 A.M.: Get up. Put clothes in the washer. Empty dishwasher. Go to office. Write. Or not. Play Solitaire. Or not.

9:30 A.M. or so: Eat breakfast. Put clothes in dryer.

10:00 A.M. – Noon: Write. Or not. Sew. Or not.

Noon – Eat lunch. Fold clothes and put them away.

12:30 P.M. – 2:00 P.M.: Do whatever I want. Fall asleep in the recliner.

2:00 P.M. – 11:00 P.M.: I'm not exactly sure what happens to the rest of the day, but it's gone.

I also volunteer, I belong to things. Much of the time, I'm busier in retirement than I ever intended to be. Productive? Not so much, and even though it's taken me eight years to figure it out, that's okay. Sometimes it's okay just to smell the roses.

40

OUT OF STEP

I'm a pleaser. I never, ever want to be the catalyst for anyone being unhappy or uncomfortable or sad. I never want to be rude (although I accomplish it fairly often—sorry!) If there is an odd number and you need an even one, I'll always be the one to opt out and go watch TV even though I hate TV. I suffer tremendous guilt over hurting someone's feelings even if—wait for it—I didn't do anything. And, no, it's not always a good thing to be.

Because pleasers get hurt way too easily. They take everything personally. They dwell on things until they drive not only themselves crazy but everyone around them, too. They can be decisive but usually aren't because, after all, what if their decision affects someone else in a negative way? They are forgiving, sometimes to the point of thinking they're probably imagining the insult they're forgiving. They can literally believe they need to be forgiven for taking something wrong.

They always say, "I don't care. Where would you like to go?" or "Where would you like to eat?" or "Whatever you want to watch." When they do make a choice, they worry incessantly that it is the wrong one. Not for themselves—they truly don't care—but for everyone else.

A pleaser will remember that in the third grade, she hurt someone's feelings for no good reason other than that she was eight years old. She will regret it for the rest of her life, even after she's apologized to the person who doesn't even remember the incident.

Pleasers can't say No. Even when they should. Even when they intend to. Even when the approval they want—and yes, we do want it, much as I hate to admit it—isn't forthcoming, they say Yes all the time because the truth of that particular matter is, they want to. They want to help, to experience, to always, always be one of the Good Guys. They want to be liked, even by people they aren't that fond of. (This whole paragraph makes me wish I knew more about psychology than I do.)

They are confused by rancor, by lies that are hurtful to people, that empathy and niceness and tolerance are seen as bad things. They don't understand bullying but don't always recognize it, either—what if someone just took it wrong? They never see situations in black-and-white—there are always shades of gray in there.

Chances are good that if you're a pleaser, you're not much of a leader. You're probably more of a follower, somewhere near the back, not quite keeping up. That's part of the problem, too, when there *is* a problem. Pleasers hate conflict, yet they never really fit into either side of an altercation, either, so they're constantly out of step.

I think a lot about changing myself. Everyone does, don't they? The political climate has made being a pleaser even more painful than it might be otherwise. But it's also made me realize a few things.

There's nothing wrong with being a pleaser. It doesn't mean you're weak, or not intelligent, or in any way pathetic. It doesn't mean you can't stand your ground if you need to or that your opinion is less important than anyone else's. A pleaser isn't necessarily a doormat. As far as not being a leader—I'm pretty sure I'll get some disagreement on this one—a good follower is just as important as a good leader.

So maybe I won't change that about myself. Even if I could, I'm not so sure I'd want to. I'm glad and grateful for those who *aren't* pleasers—they accomplish things that people like me never will. But I think I'm happy to be in the back and out of step. All that really means is that I'm dancing to my own tune—played quietly so that it doesn't bother anybody.

41
PRIVACY, FACEBOOK, AND ME

I was surprised to find this partial essay. I haven't changed my views about privacy in the years since I wrote it, but privacy has changed. It's easy to blame Facebook, a computer site that knows what you're thinking before you think it and tells you where to buy something you only just decided you wanted, but Facebook is a choice. I must admit, it's one I made willingly. I enjoy the pictures, the memes, the quotes, the jokes, the relationships created by prayer, the links to news stories I might otherwise miss, and the interaction with friends—both flesh-and-blood and cyber—and family.

However, those things I mention near the end of this column, being "a Christian, political, and a feminist," have opened me up to all kinds of things. They've caused me to lose friends (who, in retrospect, probably weren't), gotten me called names, and made me question myself (am I really a wicked, evil liar?). It is insane, but probably true, that social media is something else that has shaped the person I am.

And that's my fault. I give it too much power, don't I? So I'm going to take it back. If you identify with any of this rather confused ramble, I hope you do, too.

So, here it is, Privacy and Me, circa 2012.

WHILE I WAS TRYING to think of something specific that had a part in shaping the person I am, I went into the bathroom and closed the door even though there were only the two of us in the house. I read a letter from a friend in silence and put it back into its envelope without offering to share its contents with my husband. I wrote a blog entry. "What's it about?" Duane asked.

"Oh, you know. Stuff."

And that was when I knew.

I grew up in a very small house that held—before people starting going military and/or married—seven people, three of whom were older brothers. I say three, but it felt like many more. And it was okay. Despite being poor, we were never hungry and always had clothes to wear—though not ones as cool as everyone else's.

However, if you were looking for privacy, you were in the wrong place. I never had a door to close.

And now I do.

I remember telling my mother once that something was "none of her business." I was joking at the time, but she slapped me so hard I don't even know when my head stopped ringing. It is an unhappy memory and something I don't know that I ever fully forgave. Nor, I believe, did she fully forgive me for becoming an intensely private person. Although I never again told her something was none of her business, neither did I share my life's details with her. The more she wanted to know, the less I told. I have said before that we disappointed each other often—this was one of the ways we did so.

When I raised children—all of whom had their own rooms—they were free to keep their doors open or closed at their discretion (or lack of it.) When they married, their personal and financial lives were their own. How they raise their children is their business, not mine. My son-in-law's mother said once that we were polar opposites because they wanted to know everything about the kids' lives and we didn't want to know anything. We laughed about it and it was true to a certain point, but the absolute truth is that I never, ever want to impinge on anyone's privacy. After more than 40 years, I'm still shocked when Duane asks me to open his mail and read it.

I'm a wife, a mother, a writer. I am a Christian, political, and a feminist. No one needs to know the details of those definitions unless I'm willing to share them.

In truth, I don't think my quest for privacy is all that healthy, but I remember too well when there was no privacy at all. And I'm okay with keeping my personal doors closed.

42

RADIANCE

Sometimes you just think of words... well, of a word, and it stays with you because you like it so much. You'll find yourself using it over and over. It might be a name—I've used Jack and Kate way too many times in stories. I have a real fondness for "excruciating" and have used it in the wrong way more than once, but it just...fit somehow.

So, anyway, this morning I looked out the office window at the drizzle and the birds flying dark and noisy against the sky. I thought "pewter" might be my word of the day—it has a nice sound and it looks good spelled out. Some of those clouds are definitely pewter. But then there was a male bluebird posing on the clothesline pole, so bright he was almost iridescent. The newly mown grass is gloriously green and Bambi's descendants are walking across the yard.

I thought, oh, radiant.

Radiant? Really? That's not even a word I particularly like, for heaven's sake.

But we were at school the other night to watch *Little Women* and during the intermission we walked around the central lobby.

We peered down darkened hallways and through the glass in the doors at the lighted gymnasium where basketballs were thumping rhythmically against the floor.

At the other end of the gym, things were set up for graduation. The first word I thought of, and I've been thinking it since 1988, when our firstborn graduated, was "already." Because it all goes so fast that it's as if you never really get a chance to catch your breath and then there they are, sitting in their caps and gowns and fairly rustling with impatience to have it over. To get started on lives of their own. And in the life of parenthood, it is a moment that is no less than radiant.

Brides are almost universally glowing. Whether you watched the recent royal wedding or not, have you been able to look at the pictures of the new Duchess of Sussex without smiling back at her? I am not a weddings person, yet when I see pictures of my daughter and daughters-in-law when they got married, I am caught by the memories. And I smile back at them, too, enjoying their radiance.

I knew Bill and Mae from my earliest childhood until they passed away. They were married 60-some years. Her petite shoulder was never far from his tall one, and they looked at each other with twinkling eyes and expressions that excluded everyone else. They were radiant.

Our family suffered a loss yesterday, and I am sad—we all are. But I remember the night my mother died, when the lines of pain were magically erased from her face, and I hope it was that way for my brother. I know that he went in peace, with his son and granddaughter at his side, and while I won't pretend that death is ever painless or wonderful for those left behind, I do believe there is radiance in peace.

The sun has come up as I've written this, lending its light to the new day. I think of things to be grateful for, including time to tell people we love them. Time to hear it said back. Time to fix things that are broken or to heal if fixing isn't possible. Time to laugh in the face of pain. Even in grief there is gratitude. And radiance.

43

RED HEARTS AND MOMENTS

Recently my column had to do with being average and the virtues thereof. Reader response was great, and I'm so appreciative of that. And I'm still average and happy with it.

But today I met a friend for a several-hour work session and lunch. We talked and laughed and wrote nearly all day. On the way home, the sun was shining. It was warm but not hot. The Beach Boys' "Fun, Fun, Fun" played on the radio and I sang along —loud and terrible.

I'm in the last chapter of the book I'm writing, there was a red heart in my last text from my husband. He'd told me to be careful, because he doesn't like how I drive. And to take my time. And… you know, the red heart—it fills a well I didn't even know was running shallow.

There was nothing average about the day.

It made me think of other days. Other moments. Things like seeing just out of the corner of my eye a man with a beard like my brother's and having that broken moment of thinking he was still here. After that rush and the resulting realization of No, never again, came the recollections of growing up with him.

Memories last longer than the real thing, and you're able to edit them in your mind so that what you remember is what you need. And there it is again…the red heart. I see it with my mind's eye this time.

Memories crowd my mind faster than I can write them down. Sitting around a table with friends while my husband sings at a coffeehouse. Having family and noise in the house, deer posing prettily in the side yard, the cats sitting outside the door to the office watching me work. Conversations about kidney stones and tambourines and going back to school. Pictures decorate our lives—ones of a mountain view in North Carolina and of the eight-year-old who is the baby of the family and growing up so fast.

There are kindred spirit times. Laughing at Nan who peruses the menu studiously wherever we are and then orders the same thing every time. At my sister Nancy who reads the menu just as carefully, then says, "I'll take whatever you're having." Every time. Driving to Fort Wayne with Judy only to find out the place we're going is closed so that we end up eating on the porch of a place called "Pickles." And laughing. Always laughing.

There are times when others are unwitting in the happiness they give. Joe DeRozier every day on Facebook—the stories he tells and the magical look he gives us inside the life and work and times of a "doughnut man." When Nancy Neff laughs, deep and throaty and infectious, it's like a shot of Southern iced tea—sweet and strong and accompanied by the red heart. If Tracy's working at Dillinger's when you go in, you know you're going to get service and smiles and that you're going to feel special.

I guess that's what the red heart says. I mean, it's how we say, "I love you" when we text. It's how we say it on Valentine's Day. People who knit and crochet with Red Heart yarn are saying it with every flick of the needles or hook.

But it means more than "I love you," although that's probably enough. It means, at least for a minute or two or an afternoon, that you're special, that things are perfect, that life's scars have healed over long enough for you to take deep breaths.

It's what teachers and preachers and hospice workers do as a part of their vocations. It's what parents and siblings and best friends do—they find the moments, the red hearts, and share them. They lend strength where it's needed, balm to pain, and swatches of color to what sometimes feels like all too much black and white.

Average will always be good for me. For a lot of us, I think, but we all need flashes of the red heart. Of specialness. Of perfection.

44

THE RICKRACK CHRONICLES

I was about nine. Awkward. Not very pretty. Not good at things, not that anything held my interest for very long. We spent Thanksgiving with Great-aunt Gladys that year. She sewed the most beautiful things (notably clothes that *just fit* my Tiny Tears doll) and I told her I'd like to sew, too, but my mother wouldn't let me learn on the old treadle machine until I'd accomplished something by hand.

Did I mention I was awkward? Not the least of this was that my hands didn't do *anything* right. Aunt Gladys—that's a single "aunt," not to be confused with the double one in the paragraph above—tried teaching me to knit and gave up after a long weekend of putting in and taking out... and taking out... and taking out. But sewing? Anyone could do it, Mom thought, and you had to do it in the right order.

So Great-aunt Gladys sent me—*me*, who never got mail addressed to me unless it was my birthday—a couple of yards of green cotton print, some white rickrack, and a pattern for an apron. Since my mother wore aprons all the time, I'm pretty sure everyone thought I'd give the whole project up anyway and Mom would get a new apron out of it and the fabric wouldn't be wasted.

Well, I didn't, she did, and it wasn't.

Night after night, I stitched. I gathered, I hemmed, I added rickrack. And added it. And added it. I finished the apron. It was hideous, and I never wore aprons anyway. Did I mention I was nine? So I gave Mom the apron and she said, yes, I could learn to sew on the machine, but I didn't want to anymore. I was sick of sewing.

When I was in the seventh grade, home economics was a required course—remember that? It was half cooking and half sewing and it only took me a couple of weeks to figure out I wasn't meant to be either a chef or a seamstress. The food I cooked in class was raw in the middle and charred on the outside and the skirt I sewed was... God, it was awful. It had so many gathers in the back and so few in the front that the entire garment looked bustled. Not a good look for 1962. Did I mention I wasn't good at crafting?

I had this sister-in-law, Sadie—actually, I still have her; I'm convinced my brother married her just for me. Did I mention I'm the youngest? One year during Dollar Days, a huge Midwestern going-back-to-school event at which you could buy fabric, socks, and underwear really cheap, Sadie said, "Why don't we make some dresses?" Shifts were popular then. They were easy to make, so we did. I used Sadie's sewing machine with a knee press control and it was a lot of fun. Wonder of wonders, I was pretty good at it, too. But then shifts and sewing went out of style and I got more interested in the Beatles and other boys and I didn't sew anymore.

I grew up a child of the 60s, complete with a peace sign on a chain around my neck and folk songs echoing through my heart. I wanted a husband and children, to write books, and to help people.

I had this daughter in 1972—actually, I still have her, too. She was little and cute and so much fun to sew for that I spent years making her things. The year she was four, her dad stayed up with me on Christmas Eve until two A.M. while I made her a long Holly Hobbie dress on my horrendous old sewing machine. We drank coffee and laughed while I sewed and he assembled toys. At one point, when I was in tears because I was so tired from fighting with my sewing machine, he said, "Let me help you. You can open that big present under the tree."

But I wouldn't. I finished the dress and it was beautiful and so was she. So was the new sewing machine I unwrapped on Christmas morning. Yes, I still have the man who gave it to me, too. Did I mention a husband and children?

Twenty years later, I gave my daughter that sewing machine when I bought a new one. I used the new one sometimes, made a garment here and there, but not a lot. I had teenagers and a husband, a job and a house. I wrote stories on lined yellow paper and dreamed of being a writer. I didn't care about sewing.

In 1994, my daughter and her boyfriend called. They were engaged. Wasn't it wonderful? Would I make her wedding dress? And dresses for the three bridesmaids and the two flower girls? "Of course," I said, and from March until midnight of the day before their August wedding, I sat in the kitchen and sewed, cursed, and cried in turn.

Oh, they were gorgeous. Not the dresses so much as the girls in them. Did I mention that I wasn't very pretty? Well, I still wasn't, but oh, the beauty I'd created with the sewing machine and serger that spent all those months on the kitchen table. Twenty-five years later, I can still see the picture of them in my mind.

So I sewed for a few years. Nieces' weddings. Granddaughters' dresses. Grandsons' boxer shorts and pajamas. It was fun, but I had a job to do, books to write, bathrooms to clean. Who had time to pore over bolts of fabric and sweep up errant straight pins?

I was at a meeting when another member showed a quilt she'd made from Kaye Wood's Six-Hour Quilt pattern. They were fast and pretty and my friend gave them to the children's hospital. Gowns, too. You could whip them up in a half hour out of soft, child-friendly fabric. Oh, and turbans for cancer patients who had lost their hair. They took no time, and they helped people.

Did I mention I wanted to help people?

I turned half of my office into a sewing room—which sounds very neat, but in truth you could scarcely walk through it—and then I sewed quilts and hospital gowns and long Pioneer Day dresses for little girls who might not have them otherwise.

Even now, when writing (and, admittedly, doing other things I want) takes up most of my available time, I spend hours comparing colors and textures in fabric shops and buying from the clearance bolts at Walmart. I'm a sucker for the thread rack—all those colors!—and the notions wall. I have enough scissors that I wonder if I should have some kind of weapons license for them, and there hasn't been a sewing show created for television yet that I don't like. I love sewing machines as much as I do computers, but thankfully they do not become obsolete when next year's model comes out.

Sewing is an avocation that gives a surprising amount of sensate pleasure. The aroma of a fabric store or department, a combination of sizing and fibers, is like the scent of spring—it makes a stitcher happy, gives her energy, and opens her wallet. I'm always surprised when I buy fabric that it's not soiled from the oils of exploratory fingers. Because those of us who sew never just *look* at the material we use. We touch it, sniff it, pull out the bolt and lay it up against another to give it a critical eye. We talk across the bolts to each other.

"It'll look great till you wash it and that white border turns pink."

"The pattern calls for two yards but if you lay it the other way, you only need half that."

"It may be in the home dec department, but it'd make a great shirt."

"So what if it's ugly? It's a buck a yard and it won't look half bad with this blue."

When I look back—no matter how many times I've stopped doing it—sewing has been a constant for most of my life. The treadle machine I begged to use 50 years ago still sits in my hallway. I hated sewing on it, but I love the fact that I still have it. A Holly Hobbie dress moved from my bottom drawer to lie casually across an antique ironing board in my daughter's house. Her wedding dress hangs in the spare room closet. I remember Great-aunt Gladys sometimes, and am grateful once again for the package that came in the mail that day and the memory bank in which she opened such an expansive account for me.

Occasionally, I turn on an old movie and while away the afternoon assembling a quilt for a child who needs warmth. I hope she enjoys it. Because, whether you do it every day or once a year, sewing is all about warmth and enjoyment and making memories. It's love in every stitch.

45

THE PARENTS OF A PLAYER

I wrote this in August of 1991, when my years on bleachers were winding down, and it's been my most repeated essay ever—I put it out there every year whether readers want to see it or not. It's dated, I guess, because it's been a long time, but I still think there's very little that's better than watching your kids be engaged, whether it's in sports, band, drama, debate, or anything else. There are things I'm sorry for from my active parenting days, things I wish I'd said or done and things I wish I hadn't. But I don't regret one minute of being a spectator.

They're the parents of a player. You'll recognize them because they're the ones carrying umbrellas, rain ponchos, winter coats, a big Thirty-One bag full of blankets, and enough money for the entire family to stuff themselves on popcorn and Spanish hot dogs and nachos because there wasn't enough time for supper before the game.

They bring the weather gear even on a clear night, you'll notice, because although clouds may burst with bucketsful of rain or snow or both, the parents won't have the option of going home or even to the car. It doesn't matter if everyone else leaves the stands—as long as the players are on the field, their parents are in the bleachers.

She's the mother of a player. You'll recognize her because she's the one whose chin wobbles and whose eyes get big when someone screams at the player she belongs to. She's the one who only claps politely when her son's name is called in the team lineup because she doesn't want anyone teasing her about being unduly biased.

She's the one who, when her son does something wonderful on the field, comes completely unglued and spills popcorn and extra blankets all over the people below her on the bleachers as she jumps up and down and screams, "Way to go, honey!"

She's the mother of a player. You'll recognize her because when a player is down, regardless of who it is, she grows silent and covers her mouth with her hand and swallows hard. She's the one who says, "Is he all right? Is he getting up?" in a whisper heard all around. She's the one who, when he gets up and is fine, is first to clap her hands and laugh breathlessly and shake the fearful moisture from her eyes.

She's the mother of a player. You'll recognize her at the grocery store at five in the morning in her sweats buying food so her son can eat in that twilight time between school and game that is his own. She's the one who has washed uniforms 10,000 times and would cheerfully wash them 10,000 more if it will only keep the player safe.

He's the father of a player. You'll recognize him by his hat. It will have his son's team name on the front above the bill and a number stitched somewhere over his ear. It's a silent advertisement that says, "I'm his dad."

He's the father of a player. You'll recognize him because he's the guy working in the concession stand and craning his neck to see over the customers' heads. He will interrupt his "Can I help you?" spiel with a banshee yell of, "THAT'S IT! THAT'S IT!" and then go on as if nothing had happened. But he'll be smiling real hard.

He's the father of a player. You'll recognize him as the man in the bleachers who doesn't yell very much and never criticizes a player who is not his own. Mistakes make him angry, but someone else drawing attention to those mistakes makes him angrier.

He's the father of a player. You'll recognize him by the wondering expression of fierce pride that crosses his face and by the look of pain when the kid blows it. Every parent knows that expression of agony—it's the one you wear when you'd like to draw all your child's pain into yourself so he wouldn't have to feel it. Ever.

They're the parents of a player. On Senior Night, she'll be the one with a rose and he'll be the one with his chest puffed out. And their good cheer and enthusiasm on Senior Night will seem a little quiet, a little forced, because they know it's nearly over.

They know they'll soon be able to eat regular meals on Friday nights. That they'll no longer have to spend money on things like football packages and special shoes and funny gloves. That they won't have to sit on wobbly bleachers at away games and listen to announcers who can't pronounce their son's name.

They know the extra blankets and weather gear can go way to the back of the closet and they've probably bought the last bottle of rubber cement necessary for the scrapbook.

Pretty soon, they won't be reading Saturday morning's newspaper before the ink has completely dried and sitting at the kitchen table to listen to "Coach's Corner" on the radio. And they'll be envying the parents of underclassmen who play the game because they get to do it all again next year and maybe the year after.

They're the parents of a player. You'll recognize them because they're always there. Always.

46

THREE WISHES

Okay, continued from another time, when that article about writing prompts was so much fun I thought I'd try it again. The one I chose for today was "If I had three wishes I would…" Well, duh, I'd wish for peace on earth, good will toward all, and that disease be obliterated. Wouldn't everyone?

But wait—that's way too easy. It's what we all wish for…most of us, anyway. What if those three wishes could only be about me? No world peace, no health miracles, no making everybody get along. Just three personal wishes. Easy peasy.

First off, I'd be slim. I've been slim several times in my life and I really like it a lot. I feel better that way, look better that way, and can buy clothes without paying the extra that plus-sizing requires (that whole scenario is a column for another day). I'm sure I'd have more friends if I was slim, that my husband would love me more, that the kids would… Well, no. I'm who I am whether I'm thin or not. My friends don't care, my kids don't care, and the roommate cares more about my health than my pants size. So I guess I wouldn't waste a wish on that.

Then I'd wish to write a bestseller. Or several of them. The money would be good, for sure, but I kind of like being anonymous. I don't think I'd like a zillion letters from readers any more than the nowhere-near-that number I get now. I like that when I talk to a group of people, the room is small and it becomes a conversation rather than a lecture. While it's true that I love having "USA Today Bestseller" on the covers of all my books, it's a vanity thing—I don't write any better than I did before I had it. I'd rather write better than I do, but that comes from inside, not from a wish.

I could wish to be rich, except I've never wanted to be. I've always wanted to have enough, and since I do—most months—I don't want more than that. I've never noticed that rich people are happier than others, plus they spend an inordinate amount of time just staying rich. I do wish everyone had enough, but... no, that's not about just me.

I wish I was younger. No, I don't, because that would change the whole dynamic with everyone I know. I wouldn't have experienced the 60s because I wouldn't have been there. The only way it would work is if everyone else was younger, too. Since I've been complaining loud and long about the time change ever since the powers that be brought it back, I know that for me at least, messing with time does much more harm than good. So, no, I don't wish I was younger. I'll leave time alone.

If I'd thought of it, I'd have wished to see bluebirds out my office window, but they beat me to it. They bounced up and down on the clothesline, checked out the suet feeder, and disappeared as quickly as they came. I didn't even have to use a wish.

So... I could spend the wishes on regrets, I guess. I wish I'd never said anything mean to anyone. I wish I'd never bought that 2006 Pontiac. I wish I'd always known about Green Mountain Coffee.

What? What do you mean, that's all I get? Oh. Three wishes. Right.

And that's kind of what happens, isn't it, when you spend all your thought—and your wishes—on yourself? It goes way too fast and there's not much point in it and at the end of the day, it's lonely.

So, for now at least, I'll just keep wishing for peace on earth, good will toward all, and that disease be obliterated.

Have a good week. Stay safe. Be nice to somebody.

47
TO BE ALONE

I have my own space. It's my office-slash-sewing room. I spend hours—some of them even productive!—in here every day. It's where I write. Where I sew. Where I watch Hallmark movies and sewing shows and episodes of *The West Wing*. Virginia Woolf wrote an extended essay about this very thing called "A Room of One's Own." I've quoted it several times, but I've never read the whole thing. I'm just extremely happy to have one.

It was something I dreamed of during the years of never being able to go to the bathroom by myself, of nothing ever staying where I put it, of everyone's needs being more important than mine, of working a job that no matter how much I liked it, took up too much of life. We could do it all, women said, and we could. We did then and many are doing it now. But we shouldn't. Not without help. Not without a place to just be ourselves. To be alone.

It doesn't have to be a room.

I was 19 when I sat alone on the bleachers at the softball field in Maconaquah Park. It was one of the loneliest, scaredest times of my life, but I found answers in that silent place.

I remember being very young and seeing my sister sitting on a rock a distance from the house. "Leave her alone," my mom said. I hope I did, but I'm not counting on it.

When I was small, Mom used to walk out behind the barn by herself. I always followed her. I wish I hadn't.

Sometimes it's not even a place.

My husband plays guitar and sings. He does it in public. And he does it when he's alone, for hours at a time. I used to resent that he would stop when I walked into the room. I was wrong. Just as I have my place to be alone, he needs his as well.

When my son played football in high school, the players used to walk the field before each game. I don't know what they thought while they did it or even the reason for the silent trek up and down, up and down… But they did it every time. I remember watching them once and wanting to go out there with them because, after all, I was somebody's mother—helping's what we did, right? That was why we cooked them pasta dinners on Wednesday nights and never, ever, ever missed a game. But they didn't need help, and they didn't need to talk to anyone about what they were doing or thinking. They were growing up one step at a time.

My daughter-in-law, Tahne, travels a lot in her job, which is in a profession that is still home to more men than women. It could be lonely for her, and sometimes it is, but she uses travel time as a place of her own. No matter what city she's in, she becomes a tourist during her off time, wandering from place to place without company. It is then that she is only her, not someone's wife or mother or employee or text number. It is, she says, "…empowering to be able to be alone."

There are no greater blessings than family and friends, no more fun to be had than spending time with a kindred spirit or someone whose curiosity excites yours. Nothing better than being told you're loved every day of your life and saying it back.

The other side of that coin is that there's little that's worse than being alone when you don't want to be, feeling people you love slip away from you either physically or emotionally, or not being curious about anything.

However, if you have a room of your own, or a space, or a time, or an activity with no one taking part except yourself, then you can remember that sometimes it's necessary to be your own best friend. Sometimes the place to gather strength is from within yourself.

Sammy Davis, Jr. wrote a book and a song entitled "Yes, I Can." Being in a place of your own gives you a chance to remind yourself of that. Even if you're not a loner, if you'd rather share all responsibilities, pleasures, and pains with someone else, it's good to know that if you're ever called upon to do it by yourself, you can.

Have a good week.

48

A GOOD WEEK ALTOGETHER

Actually, it was a good week altogether. Brunch at Jarrety's in Rochester with friends with laughing and a little wine and something called Rumchata that I'm pretty sure could lead me seriously astray. Him-and-me time when I took a grandson to school. Talking to or texting with my kids. Playing Farkle with Duane and laughing so hard that falling off my stool was looking real likely. Music from the Sahaidachnys (which I've managed to misspell at every opportunity) at the Elks and dinner at Dillinger's. Friends found their cat who had been missing for three months—welcome home, Louie!

For hours at a time, I have forgotten about the shooting at Marjory Stoneman Douglas High School in Parkland, Florida. I haven't grieved with the families of the 17 who died or clutched with fear when I thought about my kids and grandkids who are on high school or college campuses every single day. I haven't ached for the loss not only of lives but of innocence. I haven't done my regular answer-delete process on Facebook or G-chatted angrily with my friend Nan. I haven't cried.

But during the other hours, I've seen so many FB posts and memes this week that decry the world today. The kids today. The parents today. The teachers and preachers, the cops and the doctors, the drugs and the booze. Facebook, video games, and violent movies. The schools and churches. The conservatives blame the liberals and the liberals blame the conservatives. Households where both parents work. Single-parent families. Lack of discipline. Atheists and Christians blame each other and all kinds of people blame Muslims. Most everyone blames Congress because they did nothing or they did the wrong thing. They blame the NRA and all who support it, the hosts of *The View*, the ACLU, and the FBI.

There is, in fact, plenty of culpability to go around. And, in another fact, passing it like the proverbial buck doesn't do anyone any good at any time. I know who I blame and I also know a large percentage of you are never in a million years going to agree with me, so maybe we need to work from the things we DO agree on.

Such as Kids Are Not Supposed to Die because of violence.

Such as Something Needs to Be Done about it. We can deal with other issues later, we can argue about semantics later, we need to do this Now.

Such as it's up to all of us to get in line and Do, and we have to figure out how to do it without trampling over each other in the process. Talking's not enough.

Because how long will it be before members of those 17 families go hours at a time without crying? Without grief. Without fear. Without interminable aches where pieces of their hearts used to be. How many days will pass without laughing hard and noticing the sunset and breathing deep of air that's not saturated with pain? How long before they stop seeing empty chairs, before they stop yearning to hear beloved voices, before they can wake in the morning and be grateful to be alive.

How long before they can say and mean, *It was a good week altogether?*

49

WHAT I SAID WAS...

"I don't know what to write about," I told my husband as we drove home from eating a lunch I didn't cook—that's the best kind. "I think I sound preachy sometimes, and I don't want to do that. I'd like to write about something funny, only I'm not really feeling funny."

He nodded. He's good that way. I'm pretty sure he didn't hear me.

"I was thinking I could make it 'pick on your husband' week. What do you think? I could write about... you know... your hearing."

He took his eyes off the road long enough to scowl at me. "Not being able to hear isn't funny. It's as annoying to people who can't hear as it is to people who have to repeat themselves."

Oh, but I didn't mean... "No," I said, "I don't mean about hearing. I mean about listening. You know, well, maybe you don't because you never—but you probably don't think that's very funny, do you?"

He shook his head. He's good that way. I'm pretty sure he didn't hear me.

"The only time you hear anything first time out is when

someone besides me is doing the talking. Then you hear them every time, even if they're not even talking to you. Then you'll tell me what they said and I'll say, I know, that's what I said. And you'll say…"

"It's not funny."

Well, he sure heard me that time.

He and I laugh sometimes at our conversations, not that they would be funny to anyone else, but they are to us. And we keep them to themselves because no one would understand them and because what one of us says is safe with the other one. (At least until I'm writing a column.)

Then there are the conversations we *don't* have. They revolve around things like TV commercials, which he watches and I don't. I don't like very many shows, either, other than *Jeopardy*, but I'm really serious about not watching commercials. They're stupid, for one thing, and they last longer than the shows themselves, for another. But Duane likes them and if I don't see them, he tells me about them.

I nod my head. I'm good that way. But I don't usually hear him.

Another conversation we don't have is one that involves feelings. I am ready, willing, and eager to talk about mine and hear about his. I've been this way for at least 48 of the 48 years we've been married. He, on the other hand, is ready, willing, and eager to watch TV commercials in order to avoid talking about his feelings or, even worse, hearing about mine. He has probably been that way for that same 48 of 48 years. I'm not sure because I may not have been listening.

We eat out a lot. I'm not complaining about that. Ever. However, we have to pre-plan. It goes like this.

I say, "What do you want for supper?"

He says, "Something easy."

I say, "We're all out of that. What else?"

"I don't care. Whatever you want to have."

"I have to cook it. The least you can do is give me a suggestion." I may whine a little there.

Deep sigh. Really deep sigh, then he says, "Let's just go out."

"Okay." I'm good that way. So agreeable. "Where do you want to go?"

"I don't care. Where do you want to go?"

"It's your turn to choose." I know this. I remember it very well. I threw it in there right after I asked which car we were taking. We almost always take his, although I never remember that when I'm looking all over the parking lot for mine.

"I chose last time."

Hunger usually settles the question. Or who's still open when we finally make up our minds. Even then, when one of us finally suggests a place, the other one says, "That's where we went last time. Remember, you had…"

No, I don't remember, because he's wrong.

It's still "pick on your husband" week (don't look this up—I really did make it up). He just told me he didn't hear what I'd said because he was blowing his nose, then said, "Don't use that. Some things are private."

So, okay, you didn't hear that from me. Neither did he. He wasn't listening.

But then there are other conversations, ones we're smart enough to begin with the words, "I need for you to listen to me." They're ones that end with, "I'm always on your side," or "I love you," or "I love you more."

Sometimes you don't even have to talk. It's right there in the other person's eyes or the way they chew their thumbnail or their expression when they stare out the window at something only they can see. That's when you don't have to say a word, or hear one. All you have to do is be there.

50
WORDS

*A*s a writer, words are some of my favorite things. I love word games even though I'm not good at them. I love looking them up, using them in sentences, using ones in writing that I wouldn't use in conversation because...really, *extrapolate*? I can't even pronounce it correctly.

It's an ongoing thing. All the way back in first grade, when we got our first paperback *Dick and Jane* readers, I fell in love with words. The first word in that little gray book was *look,* and I've been overusing that word ever since. When I write a book, I have to do a global search and remove at least half of them. This shortens the book considerably, but probably helps the story.

Words can give you power, whether you realize it at the time or not. If someone tries to make you feel stupid—and they will—just add some syllables to your response. Just be sure you know what the polysyllabic rejoinders mean, or you'll sound as stupid as someone might be trying to make you feel.

Sometimes, like if you say "philatelist" instead of "stamp collector," you just sound kind of snotty. (You probably really don't, but since I'm not sure how to pronounce that, either, I just threw that in. You should hear me butcher *juxtaposition* and *numismatist*.)

I'm a fan of euphemisms, too. Of curse words that aren't quite as...cursey...as others. They probably *are*. I'm sure *freaking* is every bit as profane and intensely meant as the word it replaces, but I'm a lot more comfortable with it. So are others of us who thought the use of certain four-letter words was a certain path to hell. I mean heck.

My love of words has never lessened even as it has become harder to think of the ones I'm looking for when I talk and write. The correct term usually remains stubbornly on the tip of my tongue or locked into my keyboard, but the rightness of an expression is still like music.

What I don't love is the hijacking of words for disparaging purposes. I've been tired of being called a snowflake for a couple of years now, yet snowflakes are beautiful things, art objects within themselves, clean and bright and perfect. So maybe that's okay. If that's not how you mean it when you're talking to me... well, look it up.

The word *retard* became something ugly because of misuse. Having its second syllable appropriated to use as an epithet—*libtard* or *Dotard* anyone?—added insult to injury to a word never intended to be pejorative.

I don't love many cutesy new words, either, ones that are added to the dictionary each year because of their common use. Why can't we just use them a while and then let them fade into the wayback of our lives, never to be thought of again. Oh, yeah, *wayback* is one of those new words, even if Word doesn't know about it and scolds me with a red squiggle. It means "the area in the back of a van, station wagon, or SUV." However, I like the way I used it and the way they used it in the "wayback machine," so maybe we can add a second meaning to its definition in *Merriam-Webster*.

That's probably how people turned *snowflake* into an epithet, isn't it? They liked the way it sounded, the feelings it stirred up and hurt, the divisiveness it deepened. I wonder if it's how homosexual became *gay* and *queer* and someone long ago thought the n-word was common usage and okay.

Words will always be some of my favorite things, but putting thought with them is an even bigger favorite. We should all try it sometime.

51
BANNING BOOKS

"*Banning books gives us silence when we need speech. It closes our ears when we need to listen. It makes us blind when we need sight.*"
~~ *Stephen Chbosky*

THIS HAPPENED IN 1991. After all these years, I can hardly believe it came to pass, but it did—book-banning really happened at our school. It made me know then that the more things changed, the more they stayed the same. I said then that we had to choose our battles—we still do. I wish I was better at choosing them. I wish I'd fought this one harder.

My son came home from school the other day and told me that someone had submitted a list to the powers that be at his school, requesting that books named on that list be eliminated from the school library. Apparently, the person who made the list did not want his or her child reading those books.

That's fine by me, but don't tell my child he can't. Or the girl down the road that she can't. Or all the other kids in the school that they can't.

Books in school libraries are chosen by people who know children, like children, and want what is best for children. Their choices are not always perfect, but they are made with the people in mind who are going to be reading the books. If they chose with the idea that they were going to please everyone, their choices would be a lot easier.

But the library's shelves would be bare.

The *Bible* would be gone. Mark Twain would be gone. Judy Blume would be gone. Nathaniel Hawthorne would be gone. Dr. Seuss, Margaret Mitchell, and, of course, Stephen King would not be allowed through school doors. Because they all offend someone, sometime, somehow.

I personally don't read Stephen King's books. He scares the bejesus out of me and keeps me awake at night. So I don't read them. But I have a kid who does, and he finds things in Stephen King's writing that I can't find and don't want to take the time to look for simply because I don't like being scared. *(Note in 2017: In 2001, Stephen King wrote my favorite book on writing of all time, called* **On Writing - A Memoir of the Craft***—go figure.)*

A young lady named Christy Martin recently had a "Student View" published in the *Peru Daily Tribune* that made a lot of sense to me. It concerned the labeling and banning of certain records, most notably those by the group 2 Live Crew. The statistics quoted in the article supported informative labeling, but "banned the ban."

Books, like records, are often "insulting, repulsive, offensive, sexist, and utterly distasteful," as Miss Martin said, but it is never up to one person or one special interest group or one church congregation to decide for everyone. Let them be labeled like movies and records, if necessary, but don't try to ban them.

It is most certainly within parents' rights to demand that their children not be required to read material they do not approve of and it is the school's responsibility to honor these demands, but let it stop there.

My children all read Robert Cormier's *The Chocolate War* in school. I read it when they did, all three times, and never did learn to like it, but they did. At least one parent I know requested that his children read an alternative selection and his request was honored. It was enough.

I told my kids I didn't want anything by 2 Live Crew in the house, just as my mom never let me play the Kingsmen's "Louie, Louie" at home. I found out that a 2 Live Crew tape has been in my son's room for a couple of years now, just as "Louie, Louie" became one of my favorites. I can't help but wonder, if I'd never said a word pro or con, if my kids weren't smart enough to decide about 2 Live Crew on their own, and I can't help but wonder if Mom shouldn't have listened to the Kingsmen and to me before banning "Louie, Louie" from the house, thereby practically forcing me to embrace it as a rock-and-roll legend to be forever loved and defended.

But it is my house, and if I find 2 Live Crew offensive, it is okay for me to ban it—or at least try to. If my mother thought "Louie, Louie" was a dirty song, it was all right for her to ban that in her house, too.

But not in your house. That's your business. And not in the school attended by my children. That's my business.

Added in 2020. It got done at that time. The book in question was banned because one mother didn't want it there. And, oh, my gosh, there are people who would ban *every*thing in libraries now if given the chance. Because there was a lot of ugliness in history, just as there is now. Because writing was done using the morals, ethics, and mores of the time and sometimes they stunk. Because people today are sometimes hurt by what was written then.

I think they would be more hurt by hiding the existence of the way things were then; banning the existence of those books would give way to denial of those flaws.

It would also be throwing out the good with the bad. One of my favorite authors for teenage girls was Janet Lambert, from

Crawfordsville, Indiana. I read every word she ever wrote and loved them all. I learned many things from them. Good things. But in those books, I don't recall there ever being a black person who wasn't a servant. I don't believe she would write that way today—at least, I hope she wouldn't—but reading them not only taught me good things, it made me pay attention to others that weren't so good.

Paying attention is important.

I'm not saying all books are good. I'm saying there are no limits to what you can learn if you read. And if you pay attention. What others read isn't your business, but there's no other way for you to argue points than if you're fully armed with facts and knowledge of both sides of a situation.

Like so many times now, I don't have a neat, tied-in-a-bow ending here. Just read. Learn. Inform. Have a great week. Be safe. Be nice to somebody.

52
SAYING THE RIGHT THING

A friend's husband passed away this week. He was a nice guy, a funny guy, a good guy, and the memories friends and family have of him will keep them going for a while as they work through the stages of grief. They'll laugh in the middle of long, hard days and lie awake and weeping in the middle of long, hard nights. But even then, when there seems to be no comfort for the loss, they'll remember what people said about the person they loved. And they will be comforted.

At his memorial service, mourners will tell stories about him. This is something I don't remember happening when I was a kid, although maybe it did; however, now people are invited to speak at nearly every service I attend. I've shared a few memories of people I loved, speaking quickly and sitting down so that I wouldn't cry or take up more than my share of time. I was never sure it was the right thing to do.

But it is. While I know it's true that you need to say all the right things to people when they're living, most of us don't always do it. We regret the missed chances, the phone call we didn't make, the birthday we forgot. We're sorry we didn't forgive or ask for forgiveness, give a compliment when we should have, or offer help when it was clearly needed. We should have stopped by. We wish we hadn't said…

But we can't unsay things. We can't undo the "wish I hads."

If I had it to do again, I'd say at my mom's and mother-in-law's funerals that they were the best mothers ever and that I was so grateful to have had them.

I would say my grandpa was one of the very best men I ever knew. He passed away in 1963 and he's still one of the best men I've ever known.

I'd tell everyone my father-in-law said I was the best birthday present he ever got. He was a charmer, so he may not have always meant it, but I'm still carrying it around with me.

At my dad's, I'd say I still never drive across railroad tracks with my foot on the brake and that when I drove a car with a standard shift, I made a conscious effort not to ride the clutch.

At Aunt Gladys's, I'd tell everyone that this very conservative, religious unmarried lady used to spend some of her lunch hours in a pool hall "during the war," (that would be the Big One, World War II), and she called other drivers "damn dummies" long before the term "road rage" was coined.

I know now that there is no "right thing" to say to mourners. They've lost someone, they're sad, and they may be angry. There may be relief that the suffering has ended or shock and bewilderment if the death was sudden. Saying you know just how they feel even if you've had a similar loss is never the right thing. You're not them in that moment, so no, you don't.

But you can talk about the ones they've loved and lost. Not just at their funerals, but afterward, too. To not say their names, even when you're trying to assuage pain by avoiding it, feels like erasure of lives that mattered. It dims the memories and stills the laughter that are left in the wake of a loved one's passing.

So, yes, when someone asks if you'd like to say something about the person whose life is being celebrated, do it. Not for the one who's gone but for those who survive him or her. The stories you tell are like gifts that never have to be given back, never wear out, and spread joy every time they're told. And if they make people laugh and cry at the same time… well, there's nothing wrong with that, either.

For Moe, in memory of Rich. I hope the stories go on for a long time.

53

THERE'S SMART... AND THEN THERE'S SMART

I'm smart.

There, I've said it. Yes, I am. Even at my age, I spell well. My grammar is adventurous but usually correct. I almost always know when to start a new paragraph, what to capitalize, and what verb tense to use. I know the Oxford comma rules the day and that the term "I seen" needs to be drummed from the English language. What I don't understand, I know how to look up—*The Chicago Manual of Style* and Google are among my very best friends.

Along that same line, I get the news from more than one source and try never to quote anything I haven't fact-checked. If I do—and it does happen—I correct myself and grovel. A little groveling, in case you didn't know, is good for everyone. If I've put up an incorrect post on Facebook, I take it down or correct it. And, yes, grovel. If someone cares to call me a liar or a snowflake because they don't like what I say, I bristle a lot, call them silent names that are much harder to spell than those, and subside, breathing deeply and thinking of karma. Oh, yes, karma.

So, yes, thank you very much, I'm smart.

Then there's mathematics. (Which I just spelled without the

"e" in the middle—thank you, autocorrect.) I had learned multiplication, long division, fractions, and decimals by the fifth grade. I could show my work, get the right answer, and still have time to pass notes in class. I can still do all those things—although it must be admitted that my handwriting isn't very legible. However, when I show my work, my kids and grandkids look at it in stupefaction. And when they mention further mathematical processes, like algebra or…any of those others, I ask them if they'd like a cookie. Because I don't know any of it. None. My son-in-law the math teacher says I use it all the time and maybe I do, but I don't know when I'm going it.

And science. The last science class I took was first year biology in high school, which I'm pretty sure I passed because the teacher was either sorry for me or because he didn't want to have me back again the next year. To this day, I'm grateful to Gloria Beecher Dance for sharing her sketches of mitosis and meiosis. I didn't get them then—or now—but she tried.

So, does this mean I'm not smart after all? Dang!

No. It doesn't. What it means is that we're all smart about different things. No surprise there, right? But there's more to it, things we all need to remember.

Number One, my smartness is no better than yours. When you mix up their, there, and they're, I may think it is, but I'm wrong. Number one and a half is that your (note: your, not you're) learnedness is no better than mine, either. It may make you feel better to call me the grammar police and snort that it doesn't matter, but it makes you look…not smart. If I make fun of you for understanding the mathematical stuff like PEMDAS, the conventional order of operations, it makes me look even less math savvy than I am. Number Two, the biggest thing we need to take from this paragraph is a reminder to Look It Up. No matter what it is. Google has made it so easy and quick that there's no excuse for you to write to when you mean too or for me to use the wrong letters when I'm trying to remember PEMDAS.

Then there's Number Three, the one that reminds us of how much we need each other's smartness. This is a big one.

I'm a Christian and I've read—in pieces—the Bible, but to say I understand it would be a gross exaggeration of my comprehension. Studying is good and asking questions of Biblical scholars is good. Because then I get the benefit of someone else's knowledge, which is far greater than mine. I think choosing a couple of verses that suit how I feel about things and running with it isn't the way to go.

I use electricity every single day. I know some safety measures, but mostly I know how to flip light switches and plug things in. I count on people with an entirely different skill set from me to keep me from killing myself. If some of them don't know the their, there, they're thing, it certain doesn't make them less smart than me. When it comes to what's going on behind the switch plate, I want their ability, not mine.

Have you ever watched people who work with their hands? Isn't it amazing? Or artists who create a whole word with a handful of brushstrokes? Or people who prepare meals and get everything done at the exact same time? Do you know caregivers who answer the same questions over and over every day, clean messes we wouldn't want to, but whose feet hit the floor running every day because that's who they are?

What smart people they are. And you are. And I am. Being smart means respecting others' knowledge, their jobs, their beliefs, and the fact that their rights are as important as yours. It also means, for all our sakes, that when you're not sure, you should look it up.

54

ROARING INTO THE TWENTIES

It is a new decade. When you reach "a certain age," life passes you by at the velocity of a bullet, but I can't say I'm all that sorry to see the old one go. I'm also pretty worried about what this next one is going to bring. I'm even more worried about what we're going to do with it, because I don't think we did so well from 2010-2019.

Like the internet. I love the internet. It is, when it comes to research, a writer's best friend. Without leaving your seat, you can find out what song was popular in 1990, the lyrics to said song, and when it's genetically possible to have blue eyes. You can also check on whether things are true or not, thanks to the unhappy necessity for fact-finders. I know the internet isn't a product of the last decade, but I believe its unfiltered access to "Hey, let's see who we can hurt today" probably is.

Then there's medication. Once again, I realize its high prices aren't a product of the last decade—maybe—but I believe the highway robbery part of it is. I'm relieved that Narcan is available free for people who have overdosed, whether accidentally or because they're trying to kill themselves. I'd be a lot more grateful if insulin and cancer drugs were free, too, or at least affordable to everyone who needs them. These people want to live and live well, yet that choice is being taken from them.

As a Christian, I've found the last decade discouraging. How can so many of us believe in the same Savior, in the same Bible, in the same ideology, and yet...not? I don't have any answers to this other than I'm almost certain calling each other bad names isn't one. I'm not sure how people in other religions feel, which is my fault for not asking, but I can't think things are any easier for them.

Speaking of calling names, I admit to beating this horse a lot more often than is worthwhile, but that one thing coupled with a total disregard for the truth is the wedding that disturbs me more than any other. It is the only marriage outside of my own that I consider any of my business. It is the only one outside of my own that has a negative influence on my life.

The school where I received my education was a public one. It was little. Flawed. Didn't have a lot of money. We had a good time, though. We learned things. We had great teachers and ones who weren't so great. We had great students and ones who barely made it through. We had taxpayers who didn't want to pay for education because they didn't have any kids, but more of them did. We knew teachers were underpaid. Their pay was one of the things I thought my generation—the Boomers—would do better. I thought we recognized value. I thought by now education would be Affordable for All and Available to All. The last decade, at least in this state, has taken a bad situation and made it much worse.

Social media has become a circus, don't you think? It still qualifies as media (I checked) but I'm not sure it fits the norm of "social." I read some of the definitions and none of them included the words rude, threatening, vicious, or false. Of course, I'm not sure *Merriam-Webster* took Facebook into consideration when they defined the word, but there you go.

There are things from the past 10 years that have been good, too. Having stuff delivered saves hours normally spent in stores. The downside for those of us who still like pushing carts down every aisle is that Walmart and Kroger and probably others now think we work there and should check ourselves out. Since the emphasis is on saving work hours and thus compensation to labor, drones are replacing drivers in many cases. I can't imagine my poor cats' response the first time an Amazon parcel is dropped on their porch by something that looks like a big dragonfly.

Health care has new ways of helping us to regain and retain good health. There are new medications, new surgery techniques, new ideas every day. But there is still quality of life to consider—longer doesn't always mean better, and until the influence of insurance companies and corporate "bonus babies" takes a smaller share of consideration, health care's impact will be lessened.

I have once again written myself into a corner I don't know how to get out of. The truth is, I'm afraid the last decade has done that to us, too. I don't know how to get out of these corners we're in. We keep sweeping and mopping as hard as we can to clean and sharpen them, but are we tossing out the good with the bad? Answers, anyone?

I hope so. I hope whatever generation we're in now does better than the ones previous. I also hope they restore civility, decency, and truth, but I might be asking too much. Just as it took more than one generation to make us what we are, it will take more than one to fix us.

I hope the 20s roar again in all good ways. However it works out, have a great week. Be nice to somebody.

55

NOT FOR KEEPING

At a meeting of churchwomen this week, Rhonda Miller read a devotion about gifts we are given. It served as a good reminder that we all have gifts, that we don't get to choose what our gifts are, and that we should use them to the greater good. The reading indicated we might not always have the same ones—that they changed all the time. I must admit that was something I'd never considered.

Although I am profoundly lacking in more areas than I want to talk about here, writing has been a gift to me since my age was still in the single digits. It was not a skill that made me popular, thin, or well-dressed, and I didn't appreciate it until I was old enough to find out there was no better place for me to find a "room of my own" than between the covers of a notebook. I was older yet when I finally got the courage to share the gift by seeking publication. The first six letters of that word, you might notice, spell "public."

Making any part of yourself public can be hard, but when you are putting the gift you've been given out there for people to like or dislike is downright scary. I used to obsess over bad reviews or other negative comments about things I'd written. I saw the criticisms as personal attacks. (I still do sometimes, although for the sake of this column, I don't want to admit it.) I equated someone not liking what I wrote to not liking me. "They don't even know me," I said, and it's true that they didn't. They did, however, know my gift because, after all, right there it was in black and white. I am so grateful to the ones who have liked the things I've written and also to the ones who haven't. My point in making my writing public—and it's only taken me half my life to figure this out—isn't so people will like me; my point is to have my work read.

I love watching live music. Not really concerts in huge venues where you sway back and forth with the flashlight on your phone eating up your battery, but in places where you drink coffee and share a table with people you know who want to enjoy the music as much as you do. I don't always like what I hear. Sometimes I think the singer is too loud and the instrumental accompaniment too repetitive. Occasionally, even with my acknowledged tin ear, I will hear someone slide far enough off-key to make me flinch.

I'm convinced some of the music doesn't even qualify to be called music. And I am wrong. Because, whether it sounds right to me or not, music is a gift claimed by those performers. It takes courage to share it knowing there are people like me who just don't get it and who will too often say so. Who will too often think that because they don't get it, it must be bad.

I was in Gallery 15 & Studios a while back, looking at paintings and purchasing a long-admired one by Sarah Luginbill for myself. I don't have an artist's eye—it goes along with my tin ear and my two left feet—but I know when something calls to me, when it settles on my heart and takes a piece of it. Part of that knowledge makes me admit that I'm not a fan of abstract art. It doesn't matter how long I stand in front of a canvas, I just can't see or feel what the artist intended. It's like I'm looking at a stereogram—a picture within a picture; I can never see those, either.

But that night, I apparently stood long enough to get something from a large abstract canvas. The colors in it were vibrant and cohesive, and it made me feel vibrant, too. Made me feel good. The artist wasn't there, but if she had been, I think she'd probably have been pleased with that. Maybe it wasn't the message she intended to send, but the one I received was positive and joyful.

There's no better example of a gift than the one given by the bite of the quilting bug. There is endless sensory pleasure in selecting fabric, cutting it, sewing it, pressing it. (There's tearing it out, too, but that doesn't land on the pleasure spectrum.) I've written about quilting before and insisted there is love in every stitch. Spending hours upon hours making something for a specific person—especially if it's a grandchild—is such a deep emotional commitment that it's hard to explain.

I've learned through quilting that having a gift doesn't always indicate you're especially good at something—although it *can* mean exactly that. If you're not, though, it means you want to do it seriously enough that you keep on doing it after you have to tear out stitches, delete scenes in a story, or paint over what you've spent hours applying to a canvas. Being gifted isn't confined to the perfectionists among us; rather it is all about the love we have for what we're doing.

In the end, gifts—just like the material presents that share use of the word—aren't so about having them as using them and sharing them. Even if we lose them, if we wake one morning unable to write or sing or paint, we will have others to replace them; it's all a matter of finding and understanding them. And giving them away.

One more thing, with an apology because I was ending this a couple of paragraphs ago, but it's important to realize that everyone has gifts. Not all of them are obvious or big or artistic, and I'm not the only one who is "profoundly lacking in more areas than I want to talk about," but they are gifts nonetheless. I hope you enjoy yours. And remember they're not for keeping.

56

SEEDS OF AGE

I changed the bottle in my water cooler the other day and reflected a little grumpily that it won't be long before I'll have to start using smaller bottles than the five-gallon ones because the weight and awkwardness are getting hard to handle.

I've been wearing the same necklace ever since the beginning of Covid-19 because neither my husband Duane nor I can consistently manage to fasten or unfasten jewelry clasps.

When we watch *Grace and Frankie*, I nod my head the whole time—not just because it's funny but because even at its most unbelievable, it's shockingly accurate.

This morning I needed something from the shed. I found the item I was looking for and went into the house to ask Duane to go out and latch the shed door because even though I got it open, I couldn't get it closed.

Walking is the only form of exercise I like, and I like to walk two miles; however, I'm tired enough after a mile and a half that I usually just do that. I might add that the mile and a half takes me as long as the two used to take.

Our 49th anniversary was yesterday. We asked each other

questions. Would you do it again? What would you change? The truth is, any change at all—including the times that create pockmarks on any enduring relationship—would alter the path of our lives together. It might be straighter—or it might not. It might put us in a place we might like less instead of more. We agreed it wasn't a chance we'd be willing to take.

All of these things are seeds planted by time. By age. Some of them were surprising—who knew I wouldn't be able to put my own necklace on? Some, like walking slower, *were* expected. But not now. Not yet.

But I've noticed...

Water in the three-gallon bottles tastes and costs the same per gallon as the water in the five-gallon bottles.

Whatever necklace I have on has memories and love attached to it—doesn't matter which one I wear or for how long I wear it.

Grace and Frankie make no pretense at not being the age they are. That they're old doesn't lessen their funniness.

People, even ones you aren't married to, will help you with things. Maybe it's because they feel sorry for you or maybe they respect your age, or maybe people are just generally nice.

When you walk slow, you smell the flowers and hear the birds and solve problems you didn't even know you had.

Scar tissue, some of the fabric that holds 49-year marriages and other friendships together, is strong stuff. Made to last if that's what both halves want to happen.

The seeds of age are hard-won and we earn them whether we want to or not. How and where we plant them and what we do with whatever grows from them... well, that's up to us.

57
THE SIXTH TRY

I've discovered that even when I try to write about something that has nothing to do with the COVID-19 virus, or quarantine, or social distancing, it doesn't work very well. The crisis and all its accouterments are the elephant in every room. So I thought I'd just go ahead and wallow in it, write about it, talk about who and what I miss. About worrying. About fear. I've now started this paragraph five times. I've spent a lot of time wandering around thinking I should be doing something productive, so maybe that's what this is. More likely, though, it's just the sixth try at a column.

I love the wildflowers on the Nickel Plate. Today it was little starry white things and even tinier yellow ones with the occasional bold and brassy dandelion pushing its way forward, saying, "Here I am, like it or not." Today, while walking, I saw six people on bicycles. We kept our distance, nodded, smiled, and said, "Hi."

I've baked this week, banana bread and cinnamon roll bread and Grands biscuits and Weight Watchers cheesecake. I've done laundry and dishes and cooked meals and gotten out of cooking a few others simply by making a phone call and picking up some really good stuff someone else prepared. Days that are never long enough suddenly are. I am never bored, but for the first time in my adulthood I understand how some people are.

On my grandson's birthday, the third grandchild's birthday during the quarantine, we took money to him and handed it to him out the window of the car. There were no hugs involved, but everyone's heart was, so it was okay.

Writing has been interesting. I've had some days when I've written more than I sometimes accomplish in a week. There have also been hiccups. There have been paragraphs and full pages written and discarded, written and discarded, written and... sometimes on the sixth time, it takes. The paper that has published the Window went on hiatus and I feel betrayed even though I wasn't. I think that explains part of the wandering around, though. Part of the inability to complete things.

DeRozier's Bakery has been delivering doughnuts all over the place. Most area restaurants are taking orders by phone and delivering to your car when you go to pick them up. Grocery stores have special hours especially for at-risk customers. More sewing machines than I'd have thought existed in the area have sewn masks steadily since the need for them first became known.

People are being heroes everywhere we turn. Healthcare workers. Retail associates. Postal workers. Other delivery personnel. Those who are sharing accurate information not colored by politics. Performers who are giving free concerts online from their living rooms, their kitchens, their showers. Teachers who left their classrooms without saying good-bye to their kids are still reading to them from Facebook, answering questions, working on e-learning. Going to meetings on Zoom. And meetings, and meetings, and meetings...

We all worry, but the worries are different for everyone. If a nurse has children at home, how scared is she or he of taking the virus home with them? Teachers can only do so much to educate without a classroom; they can't be sure their kids are doing the work in their packets or eating regularly. Everything we buy off a shelf or receive by one delivery mode or another has been touched by human hands. Many human hands. Not everyone is careful. I worry because I'm afraid I'll never be able to hug my grandkids again. I'm afraid my husband or I will get sick and we won't get to be together.

There are words and phrases being used a lot. *Hoax. Living with fear. Social distancing. Masks. We're all in it together. Good people.* The usual people are trolling social media—telling less than the truth, calling names, denigrating others because they can. They're stirring a pot that is already boiling over with floods of fear and loneliness and not giving a damn.

We are brought to tears, some of us, by unexpected things. Vandals who stole and destroyed signs meant to honor seniors who've been robbed of the last so-much-fun months of high school. Virdie Montgomery, a principal who put 800 miles on his car so that he could visit each of his seniors. A picture of a grandson heeling in apple trees in a field. Knowing another grandboy hurt his foot. Music videos.

I've been looking for a way to finish this column, this endless sixth attempt that's much more than a single paragraph. It's hard because there aren't any solutions yet.

But we will have church in the building this week, for the first time in a long time, maintaining our distance and dispensing with greeting time. Restaurants will be open at partial capacity soon. Salons are welcoming customers back slowly, one at a time. Be safe. At least as safe as you can, for the sakes of others if not for yourself. Wear a mask even if you don't like them and don't think they'll help—they sure won't hurt.

I remember a line from a book I read in junior high days. It was *Sue Barton, Rural Nurse,* and the town of Springdale, New Hampshire had suffered the effects of a terrible storm. (I think it was a hurricane, but you can't quote me on that part.) Many of the town's residents spent the night in a church, on high ground.

When they got up in the morning, they looked down on the town and its partial ruin and up at the sky, and one of them said, in words like this but maybe not exactly, "It looks like it's going to be a good day, folks."

We're going through quite the hurricane, aren't we? Some days it feels as if the eye of it is coming straight toward us and we're going to have to find a way to climb its wall to find safety again. Other days aren't so bad. They're times of doughnuts, wildflowers, grandkids' birthdays, banana bread, and heroes. So many heroes. It's days like that when we feel like we'll be able to finish the paragraph and look around and say, "It looks like it's going to be a good day, folks."

58

BACK TO THE WOOD

I'm not a very attentive person. Well, I'm attentive, just not when and where I should be. I've said before that if I were in school now, I'd probably be diagnosed with some kind of horrifying but hopefully treatable acronym. As it is, I'm unfocused to the extreme. I would blame it on age, but that's become such a huge umbrella that I'm reluctant to push anything else under it. So I will have to think of something...

Green is muscling its way into the grass in the lawn outside my office window. It is a Yes! *moment. Birds are picking their way through. We saw a fat robin in the field yesterday. I wish he'd come into the yard as I watch—it would make the picture perfect.*

Oh, yes. I don't really know what to blame it on, or if I've always been this way. I got pretty good grades when I was a kid, but I don't remember paying that much attention in the process.

You put the lime in the coconut and drink it all up...

I have tried to improve my concentration. It would make writing much easier if I did. I sometimes wonder how I've ever completed a book when I rarely type more than a paragraph without...

Que sera, sera, what will be, will be. The future's... Farmers of

America. They had cool corduroy jackets... why don't I just stick with a nine-patch instead of trying to go all Mary Fons?

Without what? Oh, without my mind going off into a dozen different directions. To make it all more complicated, I'm a pantser, not a plotter. While my people come pretty much named and fully formed, the story itself...

The ants go marching one by one, hurrah, hurrah...

...just kind of evolves, but I'm really not sure how it happens. Many times a scene will start to map itself out as I'm falling asleep. I used to keep a pen and paper beside the bed, but there were several truths involved with that. (1) I was usually too sleepy to write the ideas down, (2) if I was awake enough, the pen was out of ink, or (3) I'd dropped the pad of paper and it was somewhere under the bed, and (4) if I got under the bed for anything, I had to go get the vacuum cleaner, because there was no possible way I could go back to sleep over that much dust.

Flowers are for the living, Mom always said, so this week I remembered to send flowers to my mother-in-law. Because she's been ill. Because I love her. Because I wish my mom was here to send them to as well.

Good Lord, what Mom would say if she saw the dust under that bed! And what was that scene all about? I know it would be a good one if I could just remember it.

Occasionally thoughts will circle around to where they are together and almost harmonious. More often they clang...

...clang, clang went the trolley...

...more like a cacophony in my head.

And I have decided this is all right. In truth, I'd like to have an orderly mind (and an orderly under-the-bed, too, but we're not going there), but I just don't think it's going to happen at this point. I remember cleaning out something one time, though I don't remember what it was—surprise!—and in the mess I was cleaning, someone had spilled a box of those little sticky-back stars teachers and parents used to give as rewards.

Oohhh, shiny.

I didn't think of it then—or maybe I did—but that's the way life and the unfocused mind are. There's a lot of clutter in both, a startling lack of direction, too much discordant noise, handwriting both across and up and down the page the way they wrote letters in days gone by.

And bright stars, and joyous walks, and music, and stories I love. It's not so bad…

Starry, starry night… he cut off his ear, for heaven's sake… tulips are up… when the red, red robin comes bob, bob, bobbin' along…

There he is. There's the robin. He left too fast for me to get the picture, but it was perfect. See? Harmony.

59
HEY, MOM...

*H*ey, Mom...

My mother died in September of 1982. She raised five children to adulthood and buried a little girl at three, something she never got over. It took having children of my own to realize that no one ever does.

She was a good housekeeper, made the best cookies and homemade bread imaginable, and had a way with potato soup. Although she worked at the instrument factory in Elkhart, Indiana until she married Dad, she didn't work outside the home again until we were grown and gone, and then she was in demand as a caregiver.

Ours was not the kind of mother-daughter relationship you normally read about. We disappointed each other often. We argued a lot. I never seemed to please her, so after while, I stopped trying. In the process of being a wife and a mother and working a job and in the process of doing that, I was a terrible daughter.

Even all these many years later, it's hard to type that. Hard to admit it. It wasn't that we never had peace. We did. We laughed together sometimes. When she was ill, I took her for treatments once in a while, though not often enough, and stopped for lunch at places she liked.

The last words I ever said to her that I was sure she heard were that I loved her and would see her later. She said, "Don't go. It's going to be so long," and those words haunt me still. Because even though she asked me to stay, I didn't.

My first book was published in 1999 and I was so excited I could hardly stand it, but I sat and held the book and cried because she hadn't lived to see it. "I wish she knew," I said to my husband, and Duane said, "She does." I hope he was right. My faith says he was, but my inner voice just reminds me that I wasn't a good daughter.

I was in my early 30s when Mom died. When my kids approached that age, I went into a private panic because what if history repeated itself? I wasn't nearly ready to leave them. I still had things to tell them, things to show them, advice to offer that they might not want but would listen to cheerfully before disregarding.

You don't stop missing your mother with the passage of time. The gap in your life that was left by her leaving doesn't fill up with other things. It loses its sharp edges, but it's still there.

Why do I suddenly feel compelled to write about my mom, something I've never done a lot of? Her birthday was in April, Mother's Day in May, the anniversary of her passing a month ago yesterday, so why now?

Because October is Breast Cancer Awareness month. It's time to make an appointment for your mammogram if you haven't already had one. If you can't afford it, call your doctor's office.

Yes, I know. A federal medical panel determined you don't really need a mammogram yet, and even if you're already getting them, they said you don't need to do it as often. I don't care. I don't care what they say. Get one anyway. I was still in my 30s when I had a biopsy. Thankfully, it was benign, but the lump showed up in the mammogram I had, not because I found it on my own.

The U. S. Postal Service sells Breast Cancer Research stamps and some of their cost goes to Breast Cancer Research. They're pretty stamps, they're a reminder to everyone who notices one on an envelope, and they help a slew of people. At least in October, you might buy a sheet. You could stop in at the post office on the way to your mammogram.

If you know someone who's doing a Breast Cancer Walk, support them. Pledge money, pledge time, make the walk yourself if you have the time, health, and resources. Breast cancer isn't just the disease of the month. Even though research and improved drugs have made its statistics somewhat less terrifying, it still manages to reach every family you know.

Yes, October is Breast Cancer Awareness month, but once it's touched your family, you're aware of it forever. Mom died in 1982, but she was ill for a long time before that. Although there were good times in the last seven years of her life, there were horrific ones, too. Even if you were a bad daughter, even if you're an incurable optimist, when you remember those horrific times and how someone you loved suffered, it twists you up with a grief you can't get enough mammograms or buy enough stamps or walk far enough to diminish.

So that's why I wrote about my mom. To help keep you aware. Maybe to talk you into making that appointment or that donation. And to tell her I'm sorry I wasn't a better daughter. If I had it to do over again, I would be. But sometimes there aren't any do-overs. I guess I wanted to remind you of that, too. Have a good week. Make that appointment. Till next time.

60

THE WHEEL'S STILL IN SPIN...

I blame it on my age that I don't like change. I say I am set in my ways, that I don't have enough brain cells left to learn new things. That...well, I say lots of things, I guess, with the comment at the top of the heap being, "I just don't like it, okay?"

Much of the time, I *do* like change. As someone who grew up without plumbing, central heating, air conditioning, or store-bought milk, believe me when I say I sometimes downright *love* change. I don't want to go back to manual typewriters, car window cranks, or black-and-white television. I never want to defrost a refrigerator, clean an oven, or wax a floor ever again.

However, I remember how many changes took place in the workplace because of greed, to get rid of employees, or because the change was going to cause a boon for someone high up in the good-old-boy network. The changes didn't improve the product, lower prices, or enrich life for anyone. They were just changes for the sake of change.

I remember when all the trees were removed from one side of the tree-lined road where my parents' house was—they'd already been removed from the other side—for the sake of widening the road. The road was never widened, but its sides certainly are naked.

Twenty-some years ago the corporation where my husband worked "enhanced" the retirement program. It was the first time I ever knew *enhance* and *rape* were synonymous.

Then there are self-checkouts. I avoid them when I can, but sometimes I really don't have the time to wait in line at one of the three registers out of 27 that Walmart opens on Sunday afternoon. When I say, Hey, those ones you do for yourself are a good thing, I so remind myself that, No, they're not. They took away jobs and human contact and—here's a word fast becoming obsolete—service.

Indie-publishing, electronic and digital publishing, and Amazon have made the business of writing books unrecognizable as the same one where my first publisher called and said, "I'm going to buy your book." Brick-and-mortar bookstores have become rare things.

Some of the things that haven't changed, i.e., the us vs. them finger-pointing between separate factions, where the money goes in traditional publishing, and appalling covers are ones many of us wish *would* go away.

But they won't.

I know I sound curmudgeonly here—remember that age I mentioned?—and maybe I am. Indie-publishing has been great for a lot of writers. Many readers (myself included) read almost exclusively on electronic devices. I buy a ton of stuff from Walmart and Amazon. Because it's easy.

I'm looking out the office window this morning. It's a view that hasn't changed, other than seasonally, for at least 30 years, and it gives me unimaginable peace. I'm so glad, even with all the changes in publishing, that I still have the best job in the world.

But I miss bookstores. And cashiers who call you by name and say thank you. And that tree-lined road.

61

CLASS OF 2020

I'm listening to the Dave Clark Five. There, in case you didn't know (or care) how old I am, is irrefutable evidence. As I listen, and maybe sing along, I remember. I remember going to movies at the Roxy and at the Times in Rochester and the State in Logansport. I saw *A Hard Day's Night* seven times—at least once in each of those theaters. I saw *Woodstock* at the Roxy, *Bonnie and Clyde* at the State. I Remember *Shindig* and *Hullabaloo* and *American Bandstand* and *Where the Action Is* on TV.

I remember Friday night basketball games and football games and convocations at school. Painting mailboxes (and ourselves) to earn money in 4-H, when we rode from house to house in the back of a pickup. Once, when we were playing outside at school, some of us sixth-grade girls asked if we could take a walk. The teacher—I think maybe he was playing baseball with the boys—must have given some absentminded approval, thinking we meant we were going to walk on the school grounds. Instead, we took off down the road. A mile later, someone came along and gave us a ride back to school. In the back of his pickup.

It was a more innocent time, of course, but it was neither as good or as bad as most of us who were around then remember it. Our music was the best that ever was—argue that if you will, but we know. We know. We remember the Beatles on *Ed Sullivan* and Elvis and Chubby Checker and… oh, we remember.

It's kind of unusual for me to look back so dreamily on those days, although I tend to wax sentimental on many of the ones that came along later. I've always liked being an adult a lot better than I did being a kid. I liked being a mom and a wife and a postal worker and a writer better than I liked being a teenager. Those are the times I cherish most in my memories.

Except, of course, for senior year.

I remember that there were only two seniors who had to ride my bus in the 1967-68 school year and I was one of them. Janie was the other one and I am so glad she was there. Jim Shambarger, for six years straight, had the locker beside mine.

It was the year our school's basketball team fought and scrapped their way to the semi-state. When none of us could talk because we just stayed hoarse from week to week from yelling. When Logansport's Berry Bowl—the old one—was stuffed with supporters. Whenever our cheerleaders did the old "Two Bits" yell, everyone in the gym stood and "hollered" except the supporters of the school our team was playing against. Even now, I remember how much fun it was. How exciting. It defined the year for North Miami's Class of '68.

Although I'd never want to go back, I still get a little ache when I think about it. When I listen to some of the songs from those days, tears push against the back of my eyes and it's a good thing I'm alone in here because I couldn't talk if my life depended on it.

Listening to "Glad All Over," I find myself thinking of Connor, my fifth grandchild, who will graduate from North Miami this year. He's done what grandkids do, gone from being a toddler to being six-foot-three in the blink of an eye. He's big. Hairy. Funny. He works and drives and knows what he wants to do. Like the rest of his grandfather's and my Magnificent Seven, he is our hearts.

Covid-19 came along and his friends and he and all the other 2020 kids missed their senior trip, their spring break trips, and getting away with the kind of stuff you get away with your last semester of your last year in school.

It shouldn't be a big thing in the scheme of things, in the overall big picture of life. But it is. It is. That ache again, for him. For his classmates. For all of the class of 2020.

They came in, this senior class, with Nine Eleven, when the nation's hearts all broke in unison. The unison didn't last long. We were back to being controversial and confrontational in no time at all. Quarreling and blaming, cheating and lying, hating and... oh, loving, too. Learning and laughing. Growing in spite of ourselves. Going on.

You, the class of '20 and the ones before you and after you—you're the best of us. You're our chance to get it right. The generation that follows you won't think you did—you'll screw up as many things as you fix. Most of us don't make the mistakes of the ones who went before us; we think up new ones of our own to make. You will, too.

But you'll still be the best of us. The brightest light in this year of dimness and pain and sorrow. The loudest laughter. The sweetest music. When anyone does the "Two Bits" cheer, we're all going to stand and holler for you because you're so good. So smart. So precious to us all.

I'm so sorry for the damage that's been done to your senior year. I know it's time that you'll never get back. But it's *not* the best time of your lives—it's just one time. There are so many better times ahead for you. Because you can do anything. Be anything. Go everywhere. Have good times and bad and survive them all.

Do you remember in the movie *Hoosiers*, when Norman Dale looked around at his team in their gold satin warmups as their hands met in the middle of their circle? Do you remember what he said?

He said, "I love you guys."

You are the circle, class of 2020. You'll make us laugh. Make us weep. Make us proud. Whether you're in gold satin, denim, or leggings, I know I'm speaking for everyone who knows you when I swipe that line and change it up a little.

We love you guys.

62

SAD ON SUNDAY, STILL SAD ON THURSDAY

I wrote this long ago, a year or so after I stopped smoking. I hesitated about putting it in this collection, but not for long. It was important then and I think it still is.

Depression wasn't something I gave a whole lot of thought to. It was something that happened to other people. Young mothers who'd just had babies and were overwhelmed by the endless and huge responsibility of it all; middle-aged men who'd lost their jobs and didn't know where to find new ones; people who'd suffered emotional losses of such magnitude I couldn't begin to imagine how they felt. Being on the self-righteous side, I also thought you only really suffered from depression if you gave into it, if you didn't outrun it with a healthy sense of humor, or if you just wanted people to feel sorry for you. Average people, people like me, didn't get depressed.

And then I stopped smoking. Aside from being self-righteous, I'm also an unmitigated coward, so I did it with medication. I didn't care; it worked, and the side-effects of the medication were minimal. I'd always said that if I didn't smoke, I'd weigh 200 pounds—not a good thing if you're short and small-boned, which

I am—and I'd suck down antidepressants like they were candy. I was joking, okay? Just kidding. Really.

Well.

I don't weigh 200 pounds, but I did gain 35 in the year after I stopped smoking, and it's still there most of the time—I discovered that chocolate chip cookies are a great replacement for nicotine. But the other thing that happened in that year was that I found out depression really does strike average people. To borrow a term I've heard often in the past three years, I hit the wall.

Since I'm one of those people who always have the symptoms described in articles about diseases (it's amazing I've lived this long!), it was no surprise that I had several of the indicators of clinical depression. You know what they are. You've read them in the doctor's office while you're waiting or at Walmart or Kroger while you're taking your blood pressure. You've read them and thought, "Hmm..." because you had a couple of them. Sometimes. But then they went away, so you were okay.

But what happens when they don't go away? What do you do when you were sad on Sunday afternoon and you're still sad at bedtime on Thursday? When you're so tired you can barely get through the day but you're sleeping way too much? Or you can't get through it because you're hardly sleeping at all? When nothing's fun anymore? When you can't see an end to feeling hopeless? When, even though you'd never consider suicide yourself—oh, of course, you wouldn't—you understand people who do?

When I hit that wall, I was one of the lucky ones in that I never for one moment thought suicide was an answer. I was seldom sleepless, never slept too much, still had fun. Sometimes. But working an eight-hour day wore me out to the point that I never really wanted to get off the couch after I got home. I looked around at my husband and kids and grandkids—even them and was bewildered because, Good Lord have mercy, how could I possibly be unhappy?

But I was. Oh, I was.

I didn't really want to start smoking again, but I knew I'd be happier if I did. What was worse—to die of lung cancer or of depression? "I don't know what to do," I told my doctor. "Maybe I need to smoke again. Just some, you know, not a lot."

"No," he said. "No. I know what to do."

So he gave me a prescription and talked to me a long time about clinical depression. "You'll be fine," he promised. "Maybe six months, maybe longer. But you'll be fine."

I hated taking Zoloft. Zoloft was for weak people, people who gave in to being sorry for themselves, people who wanted others to feel sorry for them. I'd try it for a little while, but it wasn't going to work, not on me, Mrs. Average. I hated it.

But it wasn't really so bad. Maybe six months. That should get me over the hump, and maybe I wouldn't start smoking again. I could always blame the 35 pounds on it. You know, I couldn't lose weight because I was "on medication." No one had to know I was a spineless wuss who was taking antidepressants.

Six months became two years. Not that it took me that long to feel better—that's how long it was before I got the courage up to stop taking the Zoloft. I was so afraid to stop. What if I feel that way again? I thought. I would surely die from it. But stopping was painless, and the depression is only a memory. But it's a memory that can make me miserable in a heartbeat, make me question myself if, just once, I happen to be sad on Sunday afternoon.

But I am all right, I remind myself, because by Thursday night at bedtime, I have forgotten the sadness. I feel good. No, better than good; I feel wonderful. I haven't smoked for four years and one month. And I will never, ever take any of it for granted again. It is a gift.

63

DISCOVERING PASSAGES

In the 1970s, Gail Sheehy wrote a book called *Passages*. Since it was a period of life for me that involved three children, one husband, a house, and a full-time job, I didn't read the book. It didn't sound very entertaining, and believe me, if I had the time to read in those days, I wanted the subject matter to be entertaining.

I still haven't read the book, but I do think more about passages these days. A death in our family of someone who left us too soon, before his life was even in full summer, caused some of this introspection. The births of my second, third, and fourth grandchildren in scarcely more than a year created more.

The passages make me sad.

I followed a school bus the other day and thought about all the years my kids rode a bus. For the entire 13 years I had students in this school system, they had the same driver. The bus I followed the other day didn't even slow down when it passed our house and the driver who kept my children safe all those hundreds of days—not counting the ones my little darlings skipped—has passed away.

This morning, eating breakfast in a restaurant, I watched a

father with his four children. He drank his coffee, ordered for the two youngest, kept the baby from taking unscheduled flights out of the highchair, talked with his kids, and chatted with people at other tables, all without blinking an eye.

Unless you're a caregiver or a teacher, I suppose being able to keep up with a horde of kids isn't a marketable skill when you've finished raising your family, and after a while you lose it. Somewhere, somehow, the ability to think about all those different things and keep track of reaching fingers and kicking feet while still maintaining a grip on both a coffee cup and some semblance of reality passes you by.

For all of the at least 100 years that my kids were adolescents, I thought teenagers were the smartest, neatest, funniest people in the world. The times I spent with them were some of the most productive and memory-producing years of my life. I still think spectator entertainment doesn't come any better than high school sports and that most clothing looks better on 17-year-olds than on anyone else on earth. But nowadays I catch myself thinking things like *"why doesn't he wash that hair?"* or *"I wonder if he can speak a complete sentence without using a four-letter-word"* or, worst of all, *"if that was my kid, I'd—"*

I'd what? Who am I to criticize anyone's parenting skills when I made every mistake there was to make at least once, more often two or three times? Is this what passages do? Do they turn you into a grouchy old person who forgets how things were once upon a time?

I guess, if you let them, that's exactly what they'll do.

But they can do other things, too.

I recently saw both of our sons dressed up at the same time. They wore suits, the one with a beard had it neatly trimmed, their shoes were freshly polished. While we sat, necessarily quiet, I didn't have to tell either of them to stop kicking the chair in front of him, to stop whispering, to not smack his gum, to leave his brother alone.

Their father did not have to point the finger that promised trouble later on or deliver on that promise. When we took them to lunch and they both ordered beer, I didn't feel compelled to deliver the alcohol lecture I'd perfected over the years.

When we separated later in the day, I told them, "I love you. Be careful driving home," just as I have told them since the first time they palmed a set of car keys, but the pressure was off. Although I love my children more and am prouder of them than I've ever been, they are no longer my responsibility.

And when I held my newest grandson and counted his fingers and toes as I counted my endless blessings, I looked at his wonderful, tired mother and thought about how she was just beginning.

I'm glad it's her instead of me. I'm glad that when the baby stiffens up and his face turns red and he lets out a wail, I can hand him to one of her parents and say, "Here. Do something." I'm glad that although he fits my arms like a warm and comfortable sweater, I'm not cold when I hand him back.

A few years ago, I had to drive my youngest son to his home an hour away during a snowstorm. It was black dark and the roads were getting nasty. When I let my son out of the car, he leaned back in before closing the door, looking at me in the glare of the interior light, and said, "I love you. Be careful driving home."

Did I say passages made me sad? Maybe, sometimes. And sometimes not. Sometimes the discovery that things have indeed passed can brighten a gloomy day or brighten a dark night. It might even keep you from becoming a grouchy old person who forgets too much.

64
I LOVE CHRISTMAS

I love Christmas. It is my favorite holiday for reasons both spiritual and because it is a cherished memory bank of my life. Actually, I love the whole time from Thanksgiving through Christmas. However, that five- or six-week period goes by in the blink of a geriatric eye, so I like to plan ahead.

WHAT I PLAN

- Buy wrapping paper, labels, bows, Christmas cards, seasonal paper products, Christmas fabric, and 22 pounds of candy at after-Christmas sales for something like 90% off.
- Start Christmas shopping immediately following Fourth of July fireworks.
- Begin sewing Christmas gifts. Make out schedule for the holidays since I am on deadline. Write from 6:00 A.M. till noon, sew from 4:00 P.M. till 6:00 P.M. Use other waking hours productively.

- Buy baking necessities in September so that I will have plenty of time to make cookies. Remember parchment paper.
- Early in November. Finish Christmas shopping to avoid Black Friday. Buy turkey and other Thanksgiving needs.
- Wednesday night before Thanksgiving. Go to store to buy a turkey bag because even in the best-laid plans, I forget something. Red and green M & Ms are on display. Buy some.
- Each day until Christmas, do things like wrap gifts or complete a handmade gift.
- By the Sunday night after Thanksgiving, have the tree and all decorations up, half the gifts wrapped, a few batches of cookies in the freezer.
- Enjoy the holidays! God bless us, every one!

What Actually Happens

- Buy wrapping paper, labels, bows, Christmas cards, seasonal paper products, Christmas fabric, and 22 pounds of candy at after-Christmas sales for something like 90% off. Eat the candy. Lose the rest of it.
- When my sister-in-law calls in August and asks if I have my Christmas shopping done, I call her names, hang up, and eat the M & Ms I've been stockpiling to make Christmas cookies.
- Buy more M & Ms.
- Lose them.
- Oh, fine, I ate them.
- Decide I will sew aprons for everyone for Christmas.

Lay the fabric out neatly on the cutting table. It will remain there until dust gathers on it and I forget what I was going to do with it.
- First baking day in October. Buy more M & Ms. Replace the parchment paper I've lost.
- Find the parchment paper from last year and the year before. Put it somewhere that I will remember.
- Thanksgiving Thursday, the day the holiday season begins for me. Remember the meaning of a full heart because all our kids and grands are wherever we've chosen to gather. I am never a perfectionist, but this day is truly perfect. It goes by in minutes.
- Black Friday. Go shopping because it's so much fun. Buy things no one needs but are on sale. Go home smelling like every single tester in Bath and Body Works. Show my husband the purse he just bought me for Christmas.
- Saturday after Thanksgiving. Husband can't help get tree and decorations out of the attic because of rotator cuff surgery—what an excuse!—so I do the sensible thing and buy a new tree. And some ornaments. Put tree up and discover flocked trees shed white stuff indiscriminately. Run vacuum. Run it again. Husband keeps sling on for no better reason than they told him to. Run the vacuum again.
- All of December. Try to catch up with myself.
- December 24. Finish Christmas shopping. Say "Where did the time go?" 37 times. Search frantically for the cellophane tape I know I bought. Use Band-aids to secure packages.
- December 25. Everything is perfect. I've enjoyed the holidays! God bless us, every one!

65

I BELIEVE

"*Faith is believing in things when common sense tells you not to.*"
~~ Fred, in **Miracle on 34th Street**

I'M A CHRISTIAN, so believing in and embracing the "reason for the season" was never an issue. I have three older brothers, so believing in Santa Claus *was* an issue. In short, I never did. In our house, by the time I came along, Santa was a mythological folk hero portrayed, as Susan said in *Miracle on 34th Street,* by a "nice man with a white beard." I *liked* him, I *wanted* him to be real, but I knew better. Some part of me wondered if the reason a lot of classmates got better presents than I did was that they believed in St. Nick and I didn't.

Twenty or so years later, my husband and I worked hard to keep our kids' belief in Santa alive and well. Duane even gestured over the fallow fields we drove past and assured the back seat brigade that the rows only *looked* empty—they were actually filled with bumper crops of air oats. This peculiar grain, which grows only where there are children to imagine it, is what reindeer eat that allows them to fly.

One Christmas Eve, we drove home from my family's celebration through a Christmas card display of falling snow—great fat flakes falling straight down. Although it was only late afternoon, it was dark. The car was full of gifts and goodies and excited children.

Duane saw the movement from the side in time to pump the brakes gently and slow to a crawl. Allowing the cluster of antlered deer to cross in front of us to the field on the other side of the road.

The kids fell silent. Watching.

"They'll be working tonight," said Duane.

"Uh-huh." As usual, I had a brilliant rejoinder to add to the conversation.

"Filling up on air oats before they go out," one of the kids offered.

"Uh-huh."

I know the deer were whitetail, not reindeer. I know the only thing the field produced that night was a few inches of snow. I know that Duane and I did the Santa job later on that night, laughing and wrapping and eating his cookies and drinking his milk. I *know* all that, really.

A year or two ago, I was driving somewhere with grandsons in the car. I don't remember which ones or how old they were, only that there was more than one and it was wintertime. One of the boys lifted a hand, gesturing toward the field we passed. "Look," he said. "Air oats."

I don't care what I *know*—I believe.

ABOUT LIZ FLAHERTY

Retired from the post office and married to Duane for…a really long time, *USA Today* bestselling author Liz Flaherty has had a heart-shaped adult life, populated with kids and grands and wonderful friends. She admits she can be boring, but hopes her curiosity about everyone and everything around her keeps her from it. She likes traveling and quilting and reading. And she loves writing.

Find More Books by Liz Flaherty
http://lizflaherty.net/

Follow Liz Flaherty on Social Media
Facebook ~ Twitter ~ Bookbub ~ Instagram
Goodreads ~ Pinterest ~ Newsletter Sign Up

Made in the USA
Middletown, DE
29 October 2022